# Workshop on Uphill Battles in Language Processing 2016

## Scaling Early Achievements to Robust Methods

Held at the Conference on Empirical Methods in Natural Language Processing (EMNLP 2016)



Austin, Texas, USA
5 November 2016

ISBN: 978-1-5108-3151-3

**Printed from e-media with permission by:**

Curran Associates, Inc.
57 Morehouse Lane
Red Hook, NY 12571

**Some format issues inherent in the e-media version may also appear in this print version.**



Printed by Curran Associates, Inc. (2016)

For permission requests, please contact the Association for Computational Linguistics at the address below.

Association for Computational Linguistics
209 N. Eighth Street
Stroudsburg, Pennsylvania 18360

Phone: 1-570-476-8006
Fax: 1-570-476-0860

acl@aclweb.org

**Additional copies of this publication are available from:**

Curran Associates, Inc.
57 Morehouse Lane
Red Hook, NY 12571 USA
Phone: 845-758-0400
Fax: 845-758-2633
Email: curran@proceedings.com
Web: www.proceedings.com

# Introduction

Welcome to the EMNLP 2016 Workshop on Uphill Battles in Language Processing: Scaling Early Achievements to Robust Methods.

Early researchers in Natural Language Processing had lofty goals, including getting computers to understand stories, engage in natural, cooperative dialogues with people, and translate text and speech fluently and accurately from one human language to another. While there were significant early achievements (including systems such as SHRDLU, LUNAR and COOP), the knowledge they were based on and the techniques they employed could not be scaled up for practical use.

While much of what early researchers set out to achieve has been either forgotten or sidelined in favor of what can be done by exploiting large data sets and processing power, its potential value has not gone away: There is much to be gained from recognizing not just what was said, but why; from identifying conclusions naturally drawn from what has been said and what hasn't; and from representing domains in a sufficiently rich way to reduce reliance on only what a text makes explicit. As such, we believe there can be a broad and positive impact of reviving early aspirations in the current context of large data sets and "deep" and probabilistic methods.

The workshop program is split into four panel sessions and a poster session. Each panel leads a discussion on a different area of natural language processing: document understanding, natural language generation, dialogue and speech, and language grounding. Each panel session consists of four short (10 minute) presentations, two by established researchers who carried out early work in the area, and two by more junior researchers who are known for their work on specific problems in the area. Following the presentations, workshop participants are invited to discuss challenges and potential approaches for challenges in that field. In addition, the program includes twelve research abstracts that were selected out of 16 submissions. These abstracts are presented as poster boasters at the workshop, as well as in a poster session.

Our program committee consisted of 25 researchers who provided constructive and thoughtful reviews. This workshop would not have been possible without their hard work. Many thanks to you all. We also thank the U.S. National Science Foundation for financial support. Finally, a huge thank you to all the authors who submitted abstracts to this workshop and made it a big success.

Annie, Michael, Bonnie, Mike and Luke

**Organizers:**

Annie Louis, University of Essex
Michael Roth, University of Illinois Urbana-Champaign / Saarland University
Bonnie Webber, University of Edinburgh
Michael White, The Ohio State University
Luke Zettlemoyer, University of Washington

**Program Committee:**

Omri Abend, The Hebrew University of Jerusalem
Timothy Baldwin, University of Melbourne
Nate Chambers, United States Naval Academy
Ann Copestake, University of Cambridge
Vera Demberg, Saarland University
Anette Frank, Heidelberg University
Aurelie Herbelot, University of Trento
Graeme Hirst, University of Toronto
Eduard Hovy, Carnegie Mellon University
Beata Beigman Klebanov, Educational Testing Service
Anna Korhonen, University of Cambridge
Daniel Marcu, Information Sciences Institute, USC
Katja Markert, Heidelberg University
Rada Mihalcea, University of Michigan
Hwee Tou Ng, National University of Singapore
Alexis Palmer, Heidelberg University
Manfred Pinkal, Saarland University
Sameer Pradhan, Boulder Learning
Sabine Schulte im Walde, University of Stuttgart
Jan Snajder, University of Zagreb
Swapna Somasundaran, Educational Testing Service
Manfred Stede, University of Potsdam
Joel Tetreault, Yahoo! Labs
Simone Teufel, University of Cambridge
Lucy Vanderwende, Microsoft Research

**Invited Speakers:**

James Allen, University of Rochester / IHMC
Joyce Chai, Michigan State University
Yejin Choi, University of Washington
Hal Daumé III, University of Maryland, College Park
Marie-Catherine de Marneffe, Ohio State University
David DeVault, University of Southern California

# Table of Contents

# Workshop Program

**Saturday, November 5, 2016**

**09:00–10:20 Session S1: Text Understanding**

09:00–10:20 *Invited talks, followed by discussion*
Hal Daume III, Andrew Kehler, Chris Manning, Marie-Catherine de Marneffe

**10:20–10:30 Session S2: Poster Boasters**

*An Analysis of Prerequisite Skills for Reading Comprehension*
Saku Sugawara and Akiko Aizawa

*Bridging the gap between computable and expressive event representations in Social Media*
Darina Benikova and Torsten Zesch

*Statistical Script Learning with Recurrent Neural Networks*
Karl Pichotta and Raymond Mooney

*Moving away from semantic overfitting in disambiguation datasets*
Marten Postma, Filip Ilievski, Piek Vossen and Marieke van Erp

*Unsupervised Event Coreference for Abstract Words*
Dheeraj Rajagopal, Eduard Hovy and Teruko Mitamura

*Towards Broad-coverage Meaning Representation: The Case of Comparison Structures*
Omid Bakhshandeh and James Allen

**10:30–11:00 *Coffee break***

**11:00–12:20** **Session S3: Natural Language Generation**

11:00–12:20 *Invited talks, followed by discussion*
Ioannis Konstas, Kathleen McKeown, Margaret Mitchell, Donia Scott

**12:20–12:30** **Session S4: Poster Boasters**

*DialPort: A General Framework for Aggregating Dialog Systems*
Tiancheng Zhao, Kyusong Lee and Maxine Eskenazi

*C2D2E2: Using Call Centers to Motivate the Use of Dialog and Diarization in Entity Extraction*
Ken Church, Weizhong Zhu and Jason Pelecanos

*Visualizing the Content of a Children's Story in a Virtual World: Lessons Learned*
Quynh Ngoc Thi Do, Steven Bethard and Marie-Francine Moens

*Stylistic Transfer in Natural Language Generation Systems Using Recurrent Neural Networks*
Jad Kabbara and Jackie Chi Kit Cheung

*Using Language Groundings for Context-Sensitive Text Prediction*
Timothy Lewis, Cynthia Matuszek, Amy Hurst and Matthew Taylor

*Towards a continuous modeling of natural language domains*
Sebastian Ruder, Parsa Ghaffari and John G. Breslin

**12:30–14:00** ***Lunch break***

**14:00–15:20 Session S5: Dialogue and Speech**

14:00–15:20 *Invited talks, followed by discussion*
David DeVault, Mark Liberman, Diane Litman, Amanda Stent

**15:20–16:00** ***Coffee break + poster session***

**16:00–16:30 Session S6: Poster session (continued)**

**16:30–17:50 Session S7: Grounded Language**

16:30–17:50 *Invited talks, followed by discussion*
James Allen, Joyce Chai, Yejin Choi, Mark Steedman

# An Analysis of Prerequisite Skills for Reading Comprehension

**Saku Sugawara**
The University of Tokyo
7-3-1 Hongo, Bunkyo-ku
Tokyo, Japan
sakus@is.s.u-tokyo.ac.jp

**Akiko Aizawa**
National Institute of Informatics
2-1-2 Hitotsubashi, Chiyoda-ku
Tokyo, Japan
aizawa@nii.ac.jp

## Abstract

In this paper, we focus on the synthetic understanding of documents, specifically reading comprehension (RC). A current problem with RC is the need for a method of analyzing the RC system performance to realize further development. We propose a methodology for examining RC systems from multiple viewpoints. Our methodology consists of three steps: define a set of basic skills used for RC, manually annotate questions of an existing RC task, and show the performances for each skill of existing systems that have been proposed for the task. We demonstrated the proposed methodology by annotating MCTest, a freely available dataset for testing RC. The results of the annotation showed that answering RC questions requires combinations of multiple skills. In addition, our defined RC skills were found to be useful and promising for decomposing and analyzing the RC process. Finally, we discuss ways to improve our approach based on the results of two extra annotations.

## 1 Introduction

Reading comprehension (RC) tasks require machines to understand passages and respond to questions about them. For the development of RC systems, precisely identifying what systems can and cannot understand is important. However, a critical problem is that the RC process is so complicated that it is not easy to examine the performances of RC systems.

Our present goal is to construct a general evaluation methodology that decomposes the RC process and elucidates the fine-grained performance from multiple points of view rather than based only on accuracy, which is the approach used to date. Our methodology has three steps:

1. Define a set of prerequisite skills that are required for understanding documents (Section 2.1)
2. Annotate questions of an RC task with the skills (Section 2.2)
3. Analyze the performances of existing RC systems for the annotated questions to grasp the differences and limitations of their individual performances (Section 2.3)

In Section 2, we present an example of our methodology, where we annotated MCTest (MC160 development set) (Richardson et al., 2013)[1] for Step 2 and analyzed systems by Smith et al. (2015) for Step 3. In Section 3, we present two additional annotations in order to show the outlook for the development of our methodology in terms of the classification of skills and finer categories for each skill. In Section 4, we discuss our conclusions.

## 2 Approach

### 2.1 Reading Comprehension Skills

We investigated existing tasks for RC and defined a set of basic prerequisite skills, which we refer to as *RC skills*. These are presented in Table 1.

The RC skills were defined to understand the relations between multiple clauses. Here, we assumed

[1] http://research.microsoft.com/en-us/um/redmond/projects/mctest/



*Proceedings of EMNLP 2016 Workshop on Uphill Battles in Language Processing: Scaling Early Achievements to Robust Methods*, pages 1–5, Austin, TX, November 5, 2016. ©2016 Association for Computational Linguistics

| RC skills | Freq. | Descriptions or examples | Smith no RTE | Smith RTE |
|---|---|---|---|---|
| List/Enumeration | 11.7% | Tracking, retaining, and list/enumeration of entities or states | 78.6% | 71.4% |
| Mathematical operations | 4.2% | Four basic operations and geometric comprehension | 20.0% | 20.0% |
| Coreference resolution | 57.5% | Detection and resolution of coreferences | 65.2% | 69.6% |
| Logical reasoning | 0.0% | Induction, deduction, conditional statement, and quantifier | - | - |
| Analogy | 0.0% | Trope in figures of speech, e.g., metaphor | - | - |
| Spatiotemporal relations* | 28.3% | Spatial and/or temporal relations of events | 70.6% | 76.5% |
| Causal relations* | 18.3% | Why, because, the reason, etc. | 63.6% | 68.2% |
| Commonsense reasoning | 49.2% | Taxonomic/qualitative knowledge, action and event change | 59.3% | 64.4% |
| Complex sentences* | 15.8% | Coordination or subordination of clauses | 52.6% | 68.4% |
| Special sentence structure* | 10.0% | Scheme in figures of speech, constructions, and punctuation marks | 50.0% | 50.0% |
| - | - | (Accuracy in all 120 questions) | 67.5% | 70.0% |

**Table 1:** Reading comprehension skills, their frequencies (in percentage) in MCTest (MC160 development set, 120 questions), their descriptions or examples, and the accuracies of the two systems (Smith et al., 2015) for each skill. The asterisks (*) with items represent "understanding of."

ID: MC160.dev.29 (1) multiple:
C1: The princess climbed out the window of the high tower and climbed down the south wall when her mother was sleeping.
C2: She wandered out a good ways.
C3: Finally she went into the forest where there are no electric poles but where there are some caves.
Q: Where did the princess wander to after escaping?
A: Forest

Coreference resolution:
· *She* in C2 = *the princess* in C1
· *She* in C3 = *the princess* in C1
Temporal relations:
· the actions in C1 → *wandered out ...* in C2 → *went into...* in C3
Complex sentence and special sentence structure:
· C1 = *the princess climbed out...* and [*the princess*] *climbed down...* (ellipsis)
Commonsense reasoning:
· *escaping* in Q ⇒ the actions in C1
· *wandered out* in C2 and *went into the forest* in C3 ⇒ *wander to the forest* in Q and A

**Figure 1:** Example of task sentences in MCTest and annotations with comments for verification (itemized).

that, when an RC system uses an RC skill, it must already recognize individual facts described in those clauses to which the skill relates.

There are two exceptional RC skills:

*Complex sentences* target the understanding of relations between clauses in one sentence (except those having spatiotemporal or causal meanings). Such relations have schematic or rhetorical meanings. For example, the words "and" and "or" introduce coordinating clauses (we regard them as having schematic relations). In addition, the word "although" introduces a subordinate clause that represents concession (i.e., it modifies the rhetorical meaning).

*Special sentence structure* is defined as recognizing linguistic symbols or structures in a sentence and introducing their interpretations as new facts. For example, if we take "scheme" in figures of speech, this skill deals with apposition, ellipsis, transposition, and so on. This skill also targets linguistic constructions and punctuation marks.

These two skills target a single sentence, while the other skills target multiple clauses and sentences. We did not list the skill of recognizing textual entailment (TE) because we assumed that TE involves a broad range of knowledge and inferences and is therefore a generic task itself (Dagan et al., 2006).

## 2.2 Annotation of RC Questions

We manually annotated the questions of the MC160 development set (120 questions) with the RC skills that are required to answer each question. In the annotation, we allow multiple labeling.

Because the RC skills are intended for understanding relations between multiple clauses, we excluded sentences that had no relations with others and required only simple rules for answering (e.g., mc160.dev.2 (3) Context: Todd lived in a town outside the city. Q: Where does Todd live in? A: in a town). These questions were considered to require no skills.

An example of the annotations is shown in Figure 1. The percentages of the questions in which RC skills appear are in the second column of Table 1. Some of the questions are annotated with multiple labels. The number of skills required in each question is 0 for 9.2% of the questions, 1 for 27.5%, 2 for 30.0%, 3 for 26.7%, 4 for 5.8%, and 5 for 0.8%.

### 2.3 Analysis of Existing Systems

The accuracies of the system by Smith et al. (2015) and its extension with RTE (Stern and Dagan, 2011) are represented in the last two columns of Table 1.

The results showed that adding RTE to the Smith et al. (2015)'s original system provided the most effective contribution to the skill of *complex sentences*; however, it did not affect the skills of *math operations* and *special sentence structure*. Adding RTE had a relatively small contribution to the skill of *causal relations*. This did not exactly meet our expectation because we still do not have sufficient number of annotations to determine the differences between combinations of skills.

## 3 Additional Annotations

In order to improve our methodology, we considered two questions: (i) What is the difference between distributions of RC skills in two RC tasks? (ii) Can RC skills be broken up into finer categories?

To answer these questions, here we present two additional annotations. The first treated SQuAD (Rajpurkar et al., 2016). We counted the frequencies of RC skills required in that task and compared their distribution with that of MCTest. This gave clues for establishing the ideal categorization of RC skills.

For the second, we divided the skill of *commonsense reasoning* into three subcategories and used them to annotate MCTest. This should help for a sharper definition of common sense.

### 3.1 SQuAD with RC Skills

SQuAD[2] is an RC task based on a set of Wikipedia articles. The questions are made by crowdworkers, and their answers are sure to appear in the context as a word sequence. We chose 80 questions over seven articles from the development set (v1.1) and annotated them with RC skills. Figure 2 shows an example of the annotations.

[2] http://stanford-qa.com

| RC skills | Frequency SQuAD | Frequency MCTest |
|---|---|---|
| List/Enumeration | 5.0% | 11.7% |
| Mathematical operations | 0.0% | 4.2% |
| Coreference resolution | 6.2% | 57.5% |
| Logical reasoning | 1.2% | 0.0% |
| Analogy | 0.0% | 0.0% |
| Spatiotemporal relations | 2.5% | 28.3% |
| Causal relations | 6.2% | 18.3% |
| Commonsense reasoning | 86.2% | 49.2% |
| Complex sentences | 20.0% | 15.8% |
| Special sentence structure | 25.0% | 10.0% |

**Table 2:** Reading comprehension skills and their frequencies (in percentage) in SQuAD and MCTest (MC160 development set).

The annotation results are presented in Table 2. Most questions require *commonsense reasoning*. This is because the crowdworkers were asked to avoid copying words from their context as much as possible. That is, most questions require understanding of paraphrases. Compared with MCTest, the frequencies were generally low except for a few skills. This was due to the task formulation of SQuAD. For example, because SQuAD does not involve multiple choice (a candidate answer can contain multiple entities), the skill of *list/enumeration* is not required. Additionally, except for articles on a particular person or historical event, there are fewer descriptions that require *spatiotemporal relations* than in MCTest, whose datasets mainly describe tales about characters and events for young children. On the other hand, *complex sentences* and *spacial sentence structure* appear more frequently in SQuAD than in MCTest because the documents of SQuAD are written for adults. In this way, by annotating RC tasks and comparing the results, we can see the difference in characteristics among those tasks.

### 3.2 MCTest with Commonsense Types

By referring to Davis and Marcus (2015), we defined the following three types of common sense, as given in Table 3, and annotated the MC160 development set while allowing multiple labeling. We found three questions that required multiple types.

*Lexical knowledge* focuses on relations of words or phrases, e.g., synonyms and antonyms, as in WordNet. This includes hierarchical relations of

| |
|---|
| ID: Civil_disobedience, paragraph 1, question 1<br>C1: One of its earliest massive implementations was brought about by Egyptians against the British occupation in the 1919 Revolution.<br>C2: Civil disobedience is one of the many ways people have rebelled against what they deem to be unfair laws.<br>Q: What is it called when people in society rebel against laws they think are unfair?<br>A: Civil disobedience |
| Coreference resolution:<br>· *they* in C2 = *people* in C2 (different clauses)<br>· *they* in Q = *people* in Q (different clauses)<br>Temporal relation:<br>· *people have rebelled...* in C2<br>→ *when people in society rebel...* in Q<br>Complex sentences:<br>· C2 = *one of the many ways people have* (relative clause)<br>· C2 = *Civil disobedience is... against* [the object]<br>and [it is] *what they deem to...* (relative clause)<br>· Q = *What is it called... laws*<br>and *they think* [the laws] *unfair?*<br>Commonsense reasoning:<br>· *What is it called* in Q ⇒ *Civil disobedience is*<br>· *laws they think...* in C2 = *what they deem to* in Q |

**Figure 2:** Example of task sentences (excerpted) in the development set of SQuAD and their annotations with comments for verification (itemized).

content words. Therefore, this knowledge is taxonomic and categorical.

*Qualitative knowledge* targets various relations of events, including "about the direction of change in interrelated quantities" (Davis and Marcus, 2015). In addition, this knowledge deals with implicit causal relations such as physical law and theory of mind. Note that these relations are semantic, so this type of knowledge ignores the understanding of syntactic relations, i.e., the skills of *spatiotemporal relations* and *causal relations*.

The skill of *known facts* targets named entities such as proper nouns, locations, and dates. Davis and Marcus (2015) did not mention this type of knowledge. However, we added this just in case because we considered the first two types as unable to treat facts such as a proper noun indicating the name of a character in a story.

Table 3 presents the frequencies of these types and accuracies of Smith et al. (2015)'s RTE system. Because MCTest was designed to test the capability of young children's reading, known facts were hardly required. Although not reported here, we found that

| Commonsense type | Frequency | Accuracy Smith RTE |
|---|---|---|
| Lexical knowledge | 19.2% | 67.2% |
| Qualitative knowledge | 30.8% | 67.6% |
| Known facts | 2.5% | 33.3% |

**Table 3:** Commonsense types, their frequencies (in percentage) in MCTest (MC160 development set), and accuracies by Smith et al. (2015)'s RTE system.

understanding them was more required in MC500 (e.g., days of a week). While the frequencies of the first two types were relatively high, their accuracies were comparable. Unfortunately, this meant that they were inadequate for revealing the weakness of the system on this matter. We concluded that finer classification is needed. However, the distribution of the frequencies showed that even these commonsense types can characterize a dataset in terms of the knowledge types required in that task.

## 4 Discussion and Conclusion

As discussed in Section 2.3, our methodology has the potential to reveal differences in system performances in terms of multiple aspects. We believe that it is necessary to separately test and analyze new and existing RC systems on each RC skill in order to make each system more robust. We will continue to annotate other datasets of MCTest and RC tasks and analyze the performances of other existing systems.

From the observations presented in this paper, we may be able to make a stronger claim that researchers of RC tasks (more generally, natural language understanding) should also provide the frequencies of RC skills. This will help in developing a standard approach to error analysis so that systems can be investigated for their strengths and weaknesses in specific skill categories. We can determine the importance of each skill by weighting them according to their frequencies in the test set.

## Acknowledgments

We are grateful to the anonymous reviewers for their thoughtful comments and the workshop organizers. This work was supported by JSPS KAKENHI Grant Number15H0275.

## References


Ido Dagan, Oren Glickman, and Bernardo Magnini. 2006. The PASCAL recognising textual entailment challenge. In *Machine learning challenges. evaluating predictive uncertainty, visual object classification, and recognising tectual entailment*, pages 177–190. Springer.

Ernest Davis and Gary Marcus. 2015. Commonsense reasoning and commonsense knowledge in artificial intelligence. *Communications of the ACM*, 58(9):92–103.

Pranav Rajpurkar, Jian Zhang, Konstantin Lopyrev, and Percy Liang. 2016. Squad: 100, 000+ questions for machine comprehension of text. *CoRR*, abs/1606.05250.

Matthew Richardson, J.C. Christopher Burges, and Erin Renshaw. 2013. MCTest: A challenge dataset for the open-domain machine comprehension of text. In *Proceedings of the 2013 Conference on Empirical Methods in Natural Language Processing (EMNLP)*, pages 193–203.

Lenhart K Schubert. 2015. What kinds of knowledge are needed for genuine understanding? In *IJCAI 2015 Workshop on Cognitive Knowledge Acquisition and Applications (Cognitum 2015)*.

Ellery Smith, Nicola Greco, Matko Bosnjak, and Andreas Vlachos. 2015. A strong lexical matching method for the machine comprehension test. In *Proceedings of the 2015 Conference on Empirical Methods in Natural Language Processing (EMNLP)*, pages 1693–1698. Association for Computational Linguistics.

Asher Stern and Ido Dagan. 2011. A confidence model for syntactically-motivated entailment proofs. In *Proceedings of the International Conference Recent Advances in Natural Language Processing 2011*, pages 455–462, Hissar, Bulgaria, September. RANLP 2011 Organising Committee.

Jason Weston, Antoine Bordes, Sumit Chopra, and Tomas Mikolov. 2015. Towards AI-complete question answering: a set of prerequisite toy tasks. In *Proceedings of the International Conference on Learning Representations (ICLR)*.

# Bridging the gap between computable and expressive event representations in Social Media

**Darina Benikova**
Language Technology Lab
University of Duisburg-Essen
Duisburg, Germany
darina.benikova@uni-due.de

**Torsten Zesch**
Language Technology Lab
University of Duisburg-Essen
Duisburg, Germany
torsten.zesch@uni-due.de

## Abstract

An important goal in text understanding is making sense of events. However, there is a gap between computable representations on the one hand and expressive representations on the other hand. We aim to bridge this gap by inducing distributional semantic clusters as labels in a frame structural representation.

## 1 Introduction

We experience events in our everyday life, through witnessing, reading, hearing, and seeing what is happening. However, representing events computationally is still an unsolved challenge even when dealing with well-edited text. As soon as non-standard text varieties such as Social Media are targeted, representations need to be robust against alternative spellings, information compression, and neologisms.

The aim of our envisioned project is bridging the gap between *argument-level representations* which are robustly computable, but less expressive and *frame-level representations* which are highly expressive, but not robustly computable. The distinction and the gap between the two main representation types is presented in Figure 1. On the argument-level, the event *give* and all its arguments are identified, whereas on the frame-level additional semantic role labels are assigned.

We envision a representation that enables operations such as equivalence, entailment, and contradiction. In this paper, we will focus on the equivalence operation due to space constraints. These operations are not only necessary to compress the amount of information, which is especially important in high-volume, high redundancy Social Media posts, but also for other tasks such as to analyze and understand events efficiently.

We plan to achieve building a robustly computable and expressive representation that is suited to perform the discussed operations by using Social Media domain specific clusters and topic labeling methods for the frame-labeling. We intend to evaluate the validity of our representation and approach extrinsically and application-based.

## 2 Types of representations

We distinguish between representations on two levels: (i) argument-level, which can be robustly implemented more easily, and (ii) frame-level, which is highly expressive.

**Argument-level** As shown in Figure 1, most argument representations consist of an event trigger, which is mostly a verb, and its corresponding arguments (Banarescu et al., 2013; Kingsbury and Palmer, 2003). Argument-level representations based on Social Media posts are used in applications such as e.g. creating event calendars for concerts and festivals (Becker et al., 2012) or creating overviews of important events on Twitter (Ritter et al., 2012).

**Frame-level** On this level, events are represented as frame structures such as proposed by Fillmore (1976) that built upon the argument-level, i.e. the arguments are labeled with semantic roles.

A well-known frame semantic tagger is SEMAFOR (Das, 2014).



*Proceedings of EMNLP 2016 Workshop on Uphill Battles in Language Processing: Scaling Early Achievements to Robust Methods*, pages 6–10,
Austin, TX, November 5, 2016. 

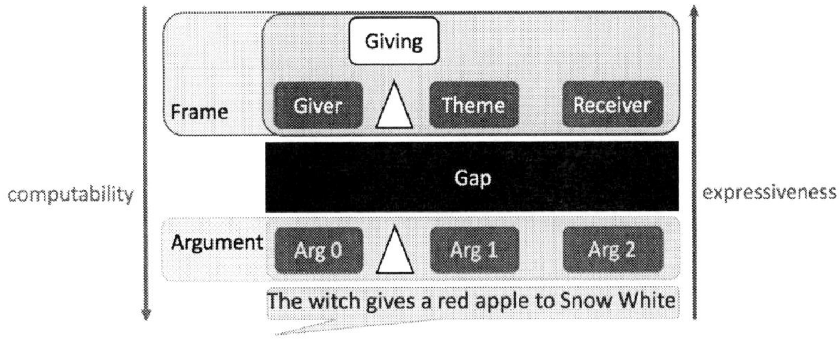


**Figure 1:** Representations of an exemplary event on argument and frame-level

## 3 Challenges

The main challenge is to bridge the gap between argument and frame-level representation.

### 3.1 Performance of operations

Our goal is to develop a representation that is both computable even on noisy Social Media text and expressive enough to support all required operations like equivalence. A semantically equivalent sentence for our examplary sentence "The witch gave an apple to Snow White" would be "Snow White received an apple from the witch.", as *receive* is the antonym of *give* and the roles of *Giver* and *Receiver* are inverted.

On the argument-level, it remains a hard problem to establish the equivalence between the two sentences, while that would be easy on the frame-level. However, getting to the frame-level is an equally hard problem and frame representations suffer from low coverage (Palmer and Sporleder, 2010).

### 3.2 Coverage

Palmer and Sporleder (2010) categorized and evaluated the coverage gaps in FrameNet (Baker et al., 2003). Coverage, whether of undefined units, lemmas, or senses, is of special importance when dealing with non-standard text that contains spelling variations and neologisms that need to be dealt with.

In our opinion, the lack of undefined units is an especially problematic issue in Social Media texts. Furthermore, it may contain innovative, informal or incomplete use of frames, due to space restrictions such as presented by Twitter. Also by cause of space restrictions, which lead to a lack of context, and considering the variety of topics that is addressed in Social Media, it is more challenging to find a fitting frame out of an existing frame repository (Ritter et al., 2012; Li and Ji, 2016).

Giuglea and Moschitti (2006) and Mùjdricza-Mayd et al. (2016) tried to bridge the gap by combing repositories on frame and argument level and representing them based on Intersective Levin Classes (ILC) (Kipper et al., 2006). ILC, which are used in VerbNet (Kipper et al., 2006), are more fine-grained than classic Levin verb classes, formed according to alternations of the grammatical expression of their arguments (Levin, 1993). Classic Levin verb classes were used for measuring semantic evidence between verbs (Baker and Ruppenhofer, 2002).

However, these approaches also have to deal with coverage problems due to their reliance on manually crafted frame repositories.

## 4 Approach

According to Modi et al. (2012) frame semantic parsing conceptually consists of 4 stages:

1. Identification of frame-evoking elements
2. Identification of their arguments
3. Labeling of frames
4. Labeling of roles

We summarize these tasks in groups of two, namely *identification* and *labeling*, and discuss our approach towards them in the following subsections.

### 4.1 Identification of frame-evoking elements and their arguments

We regard the first two tasks as tasks of the argument-level, which we plan to solve with part-of-speech tagging and dependency parsing, by extracting all main verbs to solve the first task and considering all its noun dependencies as arguments in the second task. This is similar to the approach of Modi et al. (2012).

### 4.2 Labeling of predicates and their arguments

Like Modi et al. (2012), we focus on the last two tasks, which we regard as tasks of the frame-level. We observe this task under the aspect of fitting the realization of operation tasks as discussed earlier. As we only regard predicate frames and their arguments for the role labeling, we will use *predicate* as a term for the unlabeled form of *frame* and *argument* as the unlabeled form of *role*.

**Pre-defined frame labels** There have been attempts to bridge the gap on Social Media texts by projecting ontological information in the form of computed *event types* on the event trigger on the argument-level (Ritter et al., 2012; Li et al., 2010; Li and Ji, 2016) in order to solve the task of frame labeling. However, according to Ritter et al. (2012) the automatic mapping of pre-defined event types is insufficient for providing semantically meaningful information on the event.

We aim to augment those approaches by inducing frame-like structures based on distributional semantics. Moreover, we want to use similarity clusters for the labeling of arguments in frames. We seek to compute the argument labels by the use of supersense tagging, similarly to the approach presented by Coppola et al. (2009). They successfully used the WordNet supersense labels (Miller, 1995) for verbs and nouns as a pre-processing step for the automatic labeling of frames and their arguments.

Approaches using Levin classes, ILC, or WordNet supersenses tackle the same tasks, namely labeling the frame and their corresponding roles. However, all of these suffer from the discussed coverage problem.

**Clusters as labels** To circumvent the coverage issue, there have been approaches using clusters similarly to frame labels. Directly labeling predicates and their arguments has been performed by Modi et al. (2012), who iteratively clustered verbal frames with their arguments.

As our main goal is to perform operations on event representations, we do not need human-

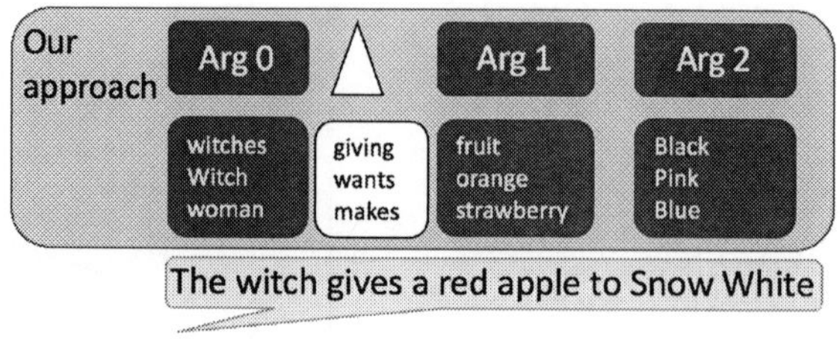


**Figure 2:** Representations of our approach to bridge the gap

readable frames as proposed by FrameNet, but a level that is semantically equivalent to it, thus our first goal is to compute domain specific clusters for the labeling.

In contrast to Modi et al. (2012), we plan to cluster the verbal predicates and the arguments separately. Although this might seem less intuitive, we believe that due to the difficulties with Social Media data, the structures of full frames are less repetitive and are more difficult to cluster. Thus, by dividing the two tasks of predicate and argument clustering, we hope to achieve better results in our setting.

Furthermore, in order to deal with the issues of the previously discussed peculiarities of the Social Media domain, we plan to train clusters on large amounts of Tweets.

An example of our envisioned representation is shown in Figure 2, which was produced using the Twitter Bigram model of JoBimViz (Ruppert et al., 2015). Figure 2 shows the clustering for finding the correct sense in the labeling task, for both the predicate and its arguments. As the example shows, this representation has some flaws that need to be dealt with. It should be mentioned that the model used for this computation is pruned due to performance reasons, which is a cause for some of the flaws.

For example, *Snow White* is not recognized as a Named Entity or a multi-word expression. To deal with the issue of the false Named Entity representation of *Snow White* presented in the exemplary representation, we plan to experiment with multi-word or Named Entity recognizers. Thus, we plan to train a similar model on a larger set of Tweets, without pruning due to performance reasons.

The main flaw is that the wrong sense cluster of *give* is selected. To improve the issues that occurred above, we plan to use soft-clustering for the step of finding the correct sense cluster. Allowing soft classes not only facilitates disambiguation (Riedl, 2016), but may also be helpful when identifying the argument role in the frame and thus allow for the previously described operations of equality. By providing only one cluster per predicate Modi et al. (2012) put the task of disambiguation aside, which we want to tackle as mentioned above.

Furthermore, aiming at representations that are suited for operations such as equality, the known problems of antonyms being in the same cluster needs to be solved. Similarly to Lobanova et al. (2010), who automatically extracted antonyms in text, we plan to solve this issue with a pattern-based approach.

**Topic-clustered labels** After succeeding in the clustering task, we plan to experiment with human-readable frame clusters. In contrast to using predefined WordNet supersenses and mapping these to frames, we want to solve the task of finding labels for the clusters by using supersenses computed from domain-specific clusters to directly label the frames and their arguments.

Our hypothesis is that by using more and soft clusters for the supersense tagging, the role labels of the event arguments become semantically richer, because more specific semantic information on the arguments and their context in the event is encoded.

Thus, we plan to use the supersense tagging by using an LDA extension, in which a combination of context and language features is used, as described by Riedl (2016).

## 5 Evaluation plan

We plan to evaluate our approach in an extrinsic, application-based way on a manual gold standard containing *event paraphrases*. In order to test how well our approach performs in comparison to state-of-the-art approaches of both *argument* and *frame representations*, such as Das (2014) or Li and Ji (2016) in the task of equivalence computation, we will compare the results of all approaches.

For this purpose, we plan to develop a dataset that is similar to Roth and Frank (2012), but tailored to the Social Media domain. They produced a corpus of alignments between semantically similar predicates and their arguments from news texts on the same event.

## 6 Summary

In this paper we present our vision on a new event representation that enables the use of operations such as equivalence. We plan to use pre-processing to get the predicates and their arguments. The main focus of the work will be using sense clustering methods on domain-specific text and to apply these clusters on text. We plan to evaluate this application in an extrinsic, application-based way.

Further on, we plan to tackle tasks such as: topic-model based frame labeling on the computed clusters; pattern-based antonym detection in the clusters for enabling the operation of contradiction and improve the task of equivalence; and experiment with Named Entity and multiword recognizers in order to improve the results in argument recognition.

## 7 Acknowledgements

This work is supported by the German Research Foundation (DFG) under grant No. GRK 2167, Research Training Group "User-Centred Social Media".

We also kindly thank the EMNLP for granting us a travel support.

## References

Collin F. Baker and Josef Ruppenhofer. 2002. FrameNet's frames vs. Levin's verb classes. In *Proceedings of the 28th annual meeting of the Berkeley Linguistics Society*, pages 27–38.

Collin F. Baker, Charles J. Fillmore, and Beau Cronin. 2003. The structure of the framenet database. *International Journal of Lexicography*, 16(3):281–296.

Laura Banarescu, Claire Bonial, Shu Cai, Madalina Georgescu, Kira Griffitt, Ulf Hermjakob, Kevin Knight, Philipp Koehn, Martha Palmer, and Nathan Schneider. 2013. Abstract Meaning Representation for Sembanking. In *Proceedings of the 7th Linguistic Annotation Workshop and Interoperability with Discourse*, pages 178–186, Sofia, Bulgaria.

Hila Becker, Dan Iter, Mor Naaman, and Luis Gravano. 2012. Identifying content for planned events across social media sites. In *Proceedings of the fifth ACM international conference on Web search and data mining*, pages 533–542, Seattle, WA, USA.

Bonaventura Coppola, Aldo Gangemi, Alfio Gliozzo, Davide Picca, and Valentina Presutti. 2009. Frame detection over the Semantic Web. In *European Semantic Web Conference*, pages 126–142. Springer.

Dipanjan Das. 2014. Statistical models for frame-semantic parsing. In *Proceedings of Frame Semantics in NLP: A Workshop in Honor of Chuck Fillmore*, pages 26–29, Baltimore, MD, USA.

Charles J. Fillmore. 1976. Frame Semantics and the Nature of Language. *Annals of the New York Academy of Sciences*, pages 20–33.

Ana-Maria Giuglea and Alessandro Moschitti. 2006. Semantic Role Labeling via FrameNet, VerbNet and PropBank. In *Proceedings of the 21st International Conference on Computational Linguistics and the 44th annual meeting of the Association for Computational Linguistics*, pages 929–936, Sydney, Australia.

Paul Kingsbury and Martha Palmer. 2003. PropBank: the Next Level of TreeBank. In *Proceedings of the Second Workshop on Treebanks and Linguistic Theories*, pages 105–116, Vaxjo, Sweden.

Karin Kipper, Anna Korhonen, Neville Ryant, and Martha Palmer. 2006. Extending VerbNet with novel verb classes. In *Proceedings of Language Resources and Evaluation*, pages 1027–1032, Genoa, Italy.

Beth Levin. 1993. *English verb classes and alternations: A preliminary investigation*. University of Chicago press.

Hao Li and Heng Ji. 2016. Cross-genre Event Extraction with Knowledge Enrichment. In *The 15th Annual Conference of the North American Chapter of the Association for Computational Linguistics: Human Language Technologies*, pages 1158–1162, San Diego, CA, USA.

Hao Li, Xiang Li, Heng Ji, and Yuval Marton. 2010. Domain-Independent Novel Event Discovery and Semi-Automatic Event Annotation. In *Proceedings of the 24th Pacific Asia Conference on Language, Information and Computation*, pages 233–242, Sendai, Japan.

Anna Lobanova, Tom Van der Kleij, and Jennifer Spenader. 2010. Defining antonymy: A corpus-based study of opposites by lexico-syntactic patterns. *International Journal of Lexicography*, 23(1):19–53.

George A Miller. 1995. WordNet: a lexical database for English. *Communications of the ACM*, 38(11):39–41.

Ashutosh Modi, Ivan Titov, and Alexandre Klementiev. 2012. Unsupervised induction of frame-semantic representations. In *Proceedings of the NAACL-HLT Workshop on the Induction of Linguistic Structure*, pages 1–7, Montral, Canada. Association for Computational Linguistics.

Eva Mùjdricza-Mayd, Silvana Hartmann, Iryna Gurevych, and Anette Frank. 2016. Combining semantic annotation of word sense & semantic roles: A novel annotation scheme for verbnet roles on german language data. In *Proceedings of the Tenth International Conference on Language Resources and Evaluation (LREC 2016)*, pages 3031–3038, Portorož, Slovenia, May.

Alexis Palmer and Caroline Sporleder. 2010. Evaluating FrameNet-style semantic parsing: the role of coverage gaps in FrameNet. In *Proceedings of the 23rd international conference on computational linguistics*, pages 928–936, Uppsala, Sweden.

Martin Riedl. 2016. *Unsupervised Methods for Learning and Using Semantics of Natural Language*. Ph.D. thesis, TU Darmstadt.

Alan Ritter, Oren Etzioni, and Sam Clark. 2012. Open domain event extraction from twitter. In *Proceedings of the 18th ACM SIGKDD international conference on Knowledge discovery and data mining*, pages 1104–1112, Beijing, China.

Michael Roth and Anette Frank. 2012. Aligning predicate argument structures in monolingual comparable texts: A new corpus for a new task. In *Proceedings of the First Joint Conference on Lexical and Computational Semantics-Volume 1: Proceedings of the main conference and the shared task, and Volume 2: Proceedings of the Sixth International Workshop on Semantic Evaluation*, pages 218–227, Montral, Canada.

Eugen Ruppert, Manuel Kaufmann, Martin Riedl, and Chris Biemann. 2015. Jobimviz: A web-based visualization for graph-based distributional semantic models. In *The Annual Meeting of the Association for Computational Linguistics (ACL) System Demonstrations*, pages 103–108.

# Statistical Script Learning with Recurrent Neural Networks

**Karl Pichotta** and **Raymond J. Mooney**
Department of Computer Science
The University of Texas at Austin
{pichotta,mooney}@cs.utexas.edu

## Abstract

We describe some of our recent efforts in learning statistical models of co-occurring events from large text corpora using Recurrent Neural Networks.

## 1 Introduction

Natural language *scripts* are structured models of stereotypical sequences of events used for document understanding. For example, a script model may encode the information that from *Smith landed in Beijing*, one may presumably infer *Smith flew in an airplane to Beijing*, *Smith got off the plane at the Beijing airport*, etc. The world knowledge encoded in such event co-occurrence models is intuitively useful for a number of semantic tasks, including Question Answering, Coreference Resolution, Discourse Parsing, and Semantic Role Labeling.

Script learning and inference date back to AI research from the 1970s, in particular the seminal work of Schank and Abelson (1977). In this work, events are formalized as quite complex hand-encoded structures, and the structures encoding event co-occurrence are non-statistical and handcrafted based on appeals to the intuitions of the knowledge engineer. Mooney and DeJong (1985) give an early non-statistical method of automatically inducing models of co-occurring events from documents, but their methods are non-statistical.

There is a growing body of more recent work investigating methods of learning statistical models of event sequences from large corpora of raw text. These methods admit scaling models up to be much larger than hand-engineered ones, while being more robust to noise than automatically learned non-statistical models. Chambers and Jurafsky (2008) describe a statistical co-occurrence model of (verb, dependency) pair events that is trained on a large corpus of documents and can be used to infer implicit events from text. A number of other systems following similar paradigm have also been proposed (Chambers and Jurafsky, 2009; Jans et al., 2012; Rudinger et al., 2015). These approaches achieve generalizability and computational tractability on large corpora, but do so at the expense of decreased representational complexity: in place of the rich event structures found in Schank and Abelson (1977), these systems model and infer structurally simpler events.

In this extended abstract, we will briefly summarize a number of statistical script-related systems we have described in previous publications (Pichotta and Mooney, 2016a; Pichotta and Mooney, 2016b), place them within the broader context of related research, and remark on future directions for research.

## 2 Methods and results

In Pichotta and Mooney (2016a), we present a system that uses Long Short-Term Memory (LSTM) Recurrent Neural Nets (RNNs) (Hochreiter and Schmidhuber, 1997) to model sequences of events. In this work, events are defined to be verbs with information about their syntactic arguments (either the noun identity of the head of an NP phrase relating to the verb, the entity identity according to a coreference resolution engine, or both). For example, the sentence *Smith got off the plane at the Beijing air-*



*Proceedings of EMNLP 2016 Workshop on Uphill Battles in Language Processing: Scaling Early Achievements to Robust Methods*, pages 11–16,
Austin, TX, November 5, 2016. 

*port* would be represented as (get_off, smith, plane, (at, airport)). This event representation was investigated in Pichotta and Mooney (2014) in the context of count-based co-occurrence models. Balasubramanian et al. (2013), Modi and Titov (2014), and Granroth-Wilding and Clark (2016) describe systems for related tasks with similar event formulations.

In Pichotta and Mooney (2016a), we train an RNN sequence model by inputting one component of an event tuple at each timestep, representing sequences of events as sequences of event components. Standard methods for learning RNN sequence models are applied to learning statistical models of sequences of event components. To infer probable unobserved events from documents, we input observed document events in sequence, one event component per timestep, and then search over the components of a next event to be inferred using a beam search. That is, the structured prediction problem of event inference is reduced to searching over probable RNN output sequences. This is similar in spirit to a number of recent systems using RNN models for structured prediction (Vinyals et al., 2015; Luong et al., 2016; Dong and Lapata, 2016).

While the count-based event co-occurrence system we investigated in Pichotta and Mooney (2014) treats events as atomic—for example, *the plane flew* and *the plane flew over land* are unrelated events with completely independent statistics—this method decomposes events into components, and the two occurrences of the verb *flew* in the above examples have the same representation. Further, a low-dimensional embedding is learned for every event component, so *flew* and *soared* can get similar representations, allowing for generalization beyond the lexical level. Given the combinatorial number of event types,[1] decomposing structured events into components, rather than treating them as atomic, is crucial to scaling up the number of events a script system is capable of inferring. In fact, the system presented in Pichotta and Mooney (2014) does not use noun information about event arguments for this reason, instead using only coreference-based entity information.

| System | Recall at 25 | Human |
|---|---|---|
| Unigram | 0.101 | - |
| Bigram | 0.124 | 2.21 |
| LSTM | 0.152 | 3.67 |

**Table 1:** Next event prediction results in Pichotta and Mooney (2016a). Partial credit is out of 1, and human evaluations are out of 5 (higher is better for both). More results can be found in the paper.

Table 1 gives results comparing a naive baseline ("Unigram," which always deterministically guesses the most common events), a co-occurrence based baseline ("Bigram," similar to the system of Pichotta and Mooney (2014)) and the LSTM system. The metric "Recall at 25" holds an event out from a test document and judges a system by its recall of the gold-standard event in its list of top 25 inferences. The "Human" metric is average crowdsourced judgments of inferences on a scale from 0 to 5, with some post hoc quality-control filtering applied. The LSTM system outperforms the other systems. More results and details can be found in Pichotta and Mooney (2016a).

These results indicate that RNN sequence models can be fruitfully applied to the task of predicting held-out events from text, by modeling and inferring events comprising a subset of the document's syntactic dependency structure. This naturally raises the question of to what extent, within the current regime of event-inferring systems trained on documents, explicit syntactic dependencies are necessary as a mediating representation. In Pichotta and Mooney (2016b), we compare event RNN models, of the sort described above, with RNN models that operate at the raw text level. In particular, we investigate the performance of a text-level sentence encoder/decoder similar to the skip-thought system of Kiros et al. (2015) on the task. In this setup, during inference, instead of encoding events and decoding events, we encode raw text, decode raw text, and then parse inferred text to get its dependency structure.[2] This system does not obviously encode event co-occurrence structure in the way that the

[1]With a vocabulary of $V$ verb types, $N$ noun types, $P$ preposition types, and event tuples of arity $k$, there are about $VPN^{k-1}$ event types. For $V = N = 10000$, $P = 50$, and $k = 4$, this is $5 \times 10^{17}$.

[2]We use the Stanford dependency parser (Socher et al., 2013).

previous one does, but can still in principle infer implicit events from text, and does not require a parser (and can be therefore be used for low-resource languages).

| System | Accuracy | BLEU | 1G P |
|---|---|---|---|
| Unigram | 0.002 | - | - |
| Copy/paste | - | 1.88 | 22.6 |
| Event LSTM | 0.023 | 0.34 | 19.9 |
| Text LSTM | 0.020 | 5.20 | 30.9 |

**Table 2:** Prediction results in Pichotta and Mooney (2016b). More results can be found in the paper.

Table 2 gives a subset of results from Pichotta and Mooney (2016b), comparing an event LSTM with a text LSTM. The "Copy/paste" baseline deterministically predicts a sentence as its own successor. The "Accuracy" metric measures what percentage of argmax inferences were equal to the gold-standard held-out event. The "BLEU" column gives BLEU scores (Papineni et al., 2002) for raw text inferred by systems (either directly, or via an intermediate text-generation step in the case of the Event LSTM output). The "1G P" column gives unigram precision against the gold standard, which is one of the components of BLEU. Figure 1, reproduced from Pichotta and Mooney (2016b), gives some example next-sentence predictions. Despite the fact that it is very difficult to predict the next sentence in natural text, the text-level encoder/decoder system is capable of learning learning some aspects of event co-occurrence structure in documents.

These results indicate that modeling text directly does not appear to appreciably harm the ability to infer held-out events, and greatly helps in inferring held-out text describing those events.

## 3 Related Work

There are a number of related lines of research investigating different approaches to statistically modeling event co-occurrence. There is, first of all, a body of work investigating systems which infer events from text (including the above work). Chambers and Jurafsky (2008) give a method of modeling and inferring simple (verb, dependency) pair-events. Jans et al. (2012) describe a model of the same sorts of events which gives superior performance on the task of held-out event prediction; Rudinger et al. (2015) follow this line of inquiry, concluding that the task of inferring held-out (verb, dependency) pairs from documents is best handled as a language modeling task.

Second, there is a body of work focusing on automatically inducing structured collections of events (Chambers, 2013; Cheung et al., 2013; Nguyen et al., 2015; Ferraro and Van Durme, 2016), typically motivated by Information Extraction tasks.

Third, there is a body of work investigating high-precision models of situations as they occur in the world (as opposed to how they are described in text) from smaller corpora of event sequences (Regneri et al., 2010; Li et al., 2012; Frermann et al., 2014; Orr et al., 2014).

Fourth, there is a recent body of work investigating the automatic induction of event structure in different modalities. Kim and Xing (2014) give a method of modeling sequences of images from ordered photo collections on the web, allowing them to perform, among other things, sequential image prediction. Huang et al. (2016) describe a new dataset of photos in temporal sequence scraped from web albums, along with crowdsourced story-like descriptions of the sequences (and methods for automatically generating the latter from the former). Bosselut et al. (2016) describe a system which learns a model of prototypical event co-occurrence from online photo albums with their natural language captions. Incorporating learned event co-occurrence structure from large-scale natural datasets of different modalities could be an exciting line of future research.

Finally, there are a number of alternative ways of evaluating learned script models that have been proposed. Motivated by the shortcomings of evaluation via held-out event inference, Mostafazadeh et al. (2016) recently introduced a corpus of crowdsourced short stories with plausible "impostor" endings alongside the real endings; script systems can be evaluated on this corpus by their ability to discriminate the real ending from the impostor one. This corpus is not large enough to train a script system, but can be used to evaluate a pretrained one. Hard coreference resolution problems (so-called "Winograd schema challenge" problems (Rahman and Ng, 2012)) provide another possible

| **Input**: | As of October 1 , 2008 , ⟨OOV⟩ changed its company name to Panasonic Corporation. |
|---|---|
| **Gold**: | ⟨OOV⟩ products that were branded "National" in Japan are currently marketed under the "Panasonic" brand. |
| **Predicted**: | The company's name is now ⟨OOV⟩. |
| **Input**: | White died two days after Curly Bill shot him. |
| **Gold**: | Before dying, White testified that he thought the pistol had accidentally discharged and that he did not believe that Curly Bill shot him on purpose. |
| **Predicted**: | He was buried at ⟨OOV⟩ Cemetery. |
| **Input**: | The foundation stone was laid in 1867. |
| **Gold**: | The members of the predominantly Irish working class parish managed to save £700 towards construction, a large sum at the time. |
| **Predicted**: | The ⟨OOV⟩ was founded in the early 20th century. |
| **Input**: | Soldiers arrive to tell him that ⟨OOV⟩ has been seen in camp and they call for his capture and death. |
| **Gold**: | ⟨OOV⟩ agrees . |
| **Predicted**: | ⟨OOV⟩ is killed by the ⟨OOV⟩. |

**Figure 1:** Examples of next-sentence text predictions, reproduced from Pichotta and Mooney (2016b). ⟨OOV⟩ is the out-of-vocabulary pseudo-token, which frequently replaces proper names.

alternative evaluation for script systems.

## 4 Future Work and Conclusion

The methods described above were motivated by the utility of event inferences based on world knowledge, but, in order to leverage large text corpora, actually model documents rather than scenarios in the world *per se*. That is, this work operates under the assumption that modeling event sequences in documents is a useful proxy for modeling event sequences in the world. As mentioned in Section 3, incorporating information from multiple modalities is one possible approach to bridging this gap. Incorporating learned script systems into other useful extrinsic evaluations, for example coreference resolution or question-answering, is another.

For the task of inferring verbs and arguments explicitly present in documents, as presented above, we have described some evidence that, in the context of standard RNN training setups, modeling raw text yields fairly comparable performance to explicitly modeling syntactically mediated events. The extent to which this is true for other extrinsic tasks is an empirical issue that we are currently exploring. Further, the extent to which representations of more complex event properties (such as those hand-encoded in Schank and Abelson (1977)) can be learned automatically (or happen to be encoded in the learned embeddings and dynamics of neural script models) is an open question.

## Acknowledgments

This research was supported in part by the DARPA DEFT program under AFRL grant FA8750-13-2-0026.

## References

Niranjan Balasubramanian, Stephen Soderland, Mausam, and Oren Etzioni. 2013. Generating coherent event schemas at scale. In *Proceedings of the 2013 Conference on Empirical Methods in Natural Language Processing (EMNLP-2013)*.

Antoine Bosselut, Jianfu Chen, David Warren, Hannaneh Hajishirzi, and Yejin Choi. 2016. Learning prototypical event structure from photo albums. In *Proceedings of the 54th Annual Meeting of the Association for Computational Linguistics (ACL-16)*.

Nathanael Chambers and Daniel Jurafsky. 2008. Unsupervised learning of narrative event chains. In *Proceedings of the 46th Annual Meeting of the Association for Computational Linguistics (ACL-08)*, pages 789–797.

Nathanael Chambers and Dan Jurafsky. 2009. Unsupervised learning of narrative schemas and their participants. In *Proceedings of the 47th Annual Meeting of the Association for Computational Linguistics (ACL-09)*, pages 602–610.

Nathanael Chambers. 2013. Event schema induction with a probabilistic entity-driven model. In *Proceedings of the 2013 Conference on Empirical Methods in Natural Language Processing (EMNLP-2013)*.

Jackie Chi Kit Cheung, Hoifung Poon, and Lucy Vanderwende. 2013. Probabilistic frame induction. In *Proceedings of the 2013 Conference of the North American Chapter of the Association for Computational Linguistics: Human Language Technologies (NAACL-13)*.

Li Dong and Mirella Lapata. 2016. Language to logical form with neural attention. In *Proceedings of the 54th Annual Meeting of the Association for Computational Linguistics (ACL-16)*.

Francis Ferraro and Benjamin Van Durme. 2016. A unified Bayesian model of scripts, frames and language. In *Proceedings of the 30th AAAI Conference on Artificial Intelligence (AAAI-16)*.

Lea Frermann, Ivan Titov, and Manfred Pinkal. 2014. A hierarchical Bayesian model for unsupervised induction of script knowledge. In *Proceedings of the 14th Conference of the European Chapter of the Association for Computational Linguistics (EACL-14)*, pages 49–57.

Mark Granroth-Wilding and Stephen Clark. 2016. What happens next? Event prediction using a compositional neural network model. In *Proceedings of the 30th AAAI Conference on Artificial Intelligence (AAAI-16)*.

Sepp Hochreiter and Jürgen Schmidhuber. 1997. Long short-term memory. *Neural Computation*, 9(8):1735–1780.

Ting-Hao K. Huang, Francis Ferraro, Nasrin Mostafazadeh, Ishan Misra, Jacob Devlin, Aishwarya Agrawal, Ross Girshick, Xiaodong He, Pushmeet Kohli, Dhruv Batra, Larry Zitnick, Devi Parikh, Lucy Vanderwende, Michel Galley, and Margaret Mitchell. 2016. Visual storytelling. In *Proceedings of the 15th Annual Conference of the North American Chapter of the Association for Computational Linguistics (NAACL-16)*.

Bram Jans, Steven Bethard, Ivan Vulić, and Marie Francine Moens. 2012. Skip n-grams and ranking functions for predicting script events. In *Proceedings of the 13th Conference of the European Chapter of the Association for Computational Linguistics (EACL-12)*, pages 336–344.

Gunhee Kim and Eric P. Xing. 2014. Reconstructing storyline graphs for image recommendation from web community photos. In *Proceedings of the 2014 IEEE Conference on Computer Vision and Pattern Recognition (CVPR-14)*.

Ryan Kiros, Yukun Zhu, Ruslan Salakhutdinov, Richard S. Zemel, Antonio Torralba, Raquel Urtasun, and Sanja Fidler. 2015. Skip-thought vectors. In *Proceedings of the 29th Annual Conference on Neural Information Processing Systems (NIPS-15)*.

Boyang Li, Stephen Lee-Urban, Darren Scott Appling, and Mark O Riedl. 2012. Crowdsourcing narrative intelligence. *Advances in Cognitive Systems*, 2:25–42.

Minh-Thang Luong, Quoc V. Le, Ilya Sutskever, Oriol Vinyals, and Lukasz Kaiser. 2016. Multi-task sequence to sequence learning. In *Proceedings of the 4th International Conference on Learning Representations (ICLR-16)*.

Ashutosh Modi and Ivan Titov. 2014. Inducing neural models of script knowledge. In *Proceedings of the Eighteenth Conference on Computational Natural Language Learning (CoNLL-2014)*, Baltimore, MD, USA.

Raymond J. Mooney and Gerald F. DeJong. 1985. Learning schemata for natural language processing. In *Proceedings of the Ninth International Joint Conference on Artificial Intelligence (IJCAI-85)*, pages 681–687.

Nasrin Mostafazadeh, Nathanael Chambers, Xiaodong He, Devi Parikh, Dhruv Batra, Lucy Vanderwende, Pushmeet Kohli, and James Allen. 2016. A corpus and cloze evaluation for deeper understanding of commonsense stories. In *Proceedings of the 2016 Conference of the North American Chapter of the Association for Computational Linguistics: Human Language Technologies (NAACL-16)*.

Kiem-Hieu Nguyen, Xavier Tannier, Olivier Ferret, and Romaric Besançon. 2015. Generative event schema induction with entity disambiguation. In *Proceedings of the 53rd Annual Meeting of the Association for Computational Linguistics (ACL-15)*.

J Walker Orr, Prasad Tadepalli, Janardhan Rao Doppa, Xiaoli Fern, and Thomas G Dietterich. 2014. Learning scripts as Hidden Markov Models. In *Proceedings of the 28th AAAI Conference on Artificial Intelligence (AAAI-14)*.

Kishore Papineni, Salim Roukos, Todd Ward, and Wei-Jing Zhu. 2002. BLEU: a method for automatic evaluation of machine translation. In *Proceedings of the 40th Annual Meeting of the Association for Computational Linguistics (ACL-02)*, pages 311–318.

Karl Pichotta and Raymond J. Mooney. 2014. Statistical script learning with multi-argument events. In *Proceedings of the 14th Conference of the European Chapter of the Association for Computational Linguistics (EACL 2014)*, pages 220–229.

Karl Pichotta and Raymond J. Mooney. 2016a. Learning statistical scripts with LSTM recurrent neural networks. In *Proceedings of the 30th AAAI Conference on Artificial Intelligence (AAAI-16)*.

Karl Pichotta and Raymond J. Mooney. 2016b. Using sentence-level LSTM language models for script inference. In *Proceedings of the 54th Annual Meeting of the Association for Computational Linguistics (ACL-16)*, Berlin, Germany.

Altaf Rahman and Vincent Ng. 2012. Resolving complex cases of definite pronouns: the Winograd schema challenge. In *Proceedings of the 2012 Conference on Empirical Methods in Natural Language Processing and Computational Natural Language Learning (EMNLP-CoNLL-12)*, pages 777–789.

Michaela Regneri, Alexander Koller, and Manfred Pinkal. 2010. Learning script knowledge with web experiments. In *Proceedings of the 48th Annual Meeting of the Association for Computational Linguistics (ACL-10)*, Uppsala, Sweden, July.

Rachel Rudinger, Pushpendre Rastogi, Francis Ferraro, and Benjamin Van Durme. 2015. Script induction as language modeling. In *Proceedings of the 2015 Conference on Empirical Methods in Natural Language Processing (EMNLP-15)*.

Roger C. Schank and Robert P. Abelson. 1977. *Scripts, Plans, Goals and Understanding: An Inquiry into Human Knowledge Structures*. Lawrence Erlbaum and Associates.

Richard Socher, John Bauer, Christopher D. Manning, and Andrew Y. Ng. 2013. Parsing with compositional vector grammars. In *Proceedings of the 51st Annual Meeting of the Association for Computational Linguistics (ACL-13)*.

Oriol Vinyals, Łukasz Kaiser, Terry Koo, Slav Petrov, Ilya Sutskever, and Geoffrey Hinton. 2015. Grammar as a foreign language. In *Proceedings of the 29th Annual Conference on Neural Information Processing Systems (NIPS-15)*, pages 2755–2763.

# Moving away from semantic overfitting in disambiguation datasets

**Marten Postma** and **Filip Ilievski** and **Piek Vossen** and **Marieke van Erp**
Vrije Universiteit Amsterdam
m.c.postma,f.ilievski,piek.vossen,marieke.van.erp@vu.nl

## Abstract

Entities and events in the world have no frequency, but our communication about them and the expressions we use to refer to them do have a strong frequency profile. Language expressions and their meanings follow a Zipfian distribution, featuring a small amount of very frequent observations and a very long tail of low frequent observations. Since our NLP datasets sample texts but do not sample the world, they are no exception to Zipf's law. This causes a lack of representativeness in our NLP tasks, leading to models that can capture the head phenomena in language, but fail when dealing with the long tail. We therefore propose a referential challenge for semantic NLP that reflects a higher degree of ambiguity and variance and captures a large range of small real-world phenomena. To perform well, systems would have to show deep understanding on the linguistic tail.

## 1 Introduction

Semantic processing addresses the relation between natural language and a representation of a world, to which language makes reference. A challenging property of this relation is the context-bound complex interaction between lexical expressions and world meanings.[1] Like many natural phenomena, the distribution of expressions and their meanings follows a power law such as Zipf's law (Newman, 2005) , with a few very frequent observations and a very long tail of low frequent observations.[2] Still, the world itself has no frequency. All entities and events in the world appear to us with a frequency of 1. Nevertheless, we dominantly talk about only a few instances in the world and refer to them with a small set of expressions, which can only be explained by the contextual constraints within a language community, a topic, a location, and a period of time. Without taking these into account, it is impossible to fully determine meaning.

Given that instances in the world do not have frequencies, language and our writing about the world is heavily skewed, selective, and biased with respect to that world. A name such as *Ronaldo* can have an infinite amount of references and in any world (real or imaginary) each *Ronaldo* is equally present. Our datasets, however, usually make reference to only one *Ronaldo*. The problem, as we see it, is that our NLP datasets sample texts but do not sample the world. This causes lack of representativeness in our NLP tasks, that has big consequences for language models: they tend to capture the head phenomena in text without considering the context constraints and thus fail when dealing with less dominant world phenomena. As a result, there is little awareness of the full complexity of the task in relation to the contextual realities, given language as a system of expressions and the possible interpretations within contexts of time, location, community, and topic. People, however, have no problem to handle local real-world situations that are referenced to in text.

We believe it is time to create a task that encour-

[1] We use *meaning* as an umbrella term for both concepts or lexical meanings and instances or entities, and *lexical expression* as a common term for both lemmas and surface forms.

[2] We acknowledge that there also exist many long tail phenomena in syntactic processing, e.g. syntactic parsing.



*Proceedings of EMNLP 2016 Workshop on Uphill Battles in Language Processing: Scaling Early Achievements to Robust Methods*, pages 17–21,
Austin, TX, November 5, 2016. 

ages systems to model the full complexity of disambiguation by enriched context awareness. We hence propose a semantic referential challenge, event-based Question Answering (QA), that reflects a high degree of ambiguity and variance and captures a wide range of small real-world phenomena. This task requires a deeper semantic understanding of the linguistic tail of several disambiguation challenges.

## 2 Related work

We present related work on the representativeness of the disambiguation datasets (Section 2.1), as well as the representativeness of the QA task (Section 2.2).

### 2.1 The Long Tail in disambiguation tasks

Past work tried to improve the disambiguation complexity. Vossen et al. (2013) created a balanced corpus, DutchSemCor, for the Word Sense Disambiguation (WSD) task in which each sense gets an equal number of examples. Guha et al. (2015) created the QuizBowl dataset for Entity Coreference (EnC), while Cybulska and Vossen (2014) extended the existing Event Coreference (EvC) dataset ECB to ECB+, both efforts resulting in notably greater ambiguity and temporal diversity. Although all these datasets increase the complexity for disambiguation, they still contain a limited amount of data which is far from approximating realistic tasks.

Properties of existing disambiguation datasets have been examined for individual tasks. For WSD, the correct sense of a lemma is shown to often coincide with the most frequent sense (Preiss, 2006). Van Erp et al. (2016) conclude that Entity Linking (EL) datasets contain very little referential ambiguity and focus on well-known entities, i.e. entities with high PageRank (Page et al., 1999) values. Moreover, the authors note a considerable overlap of entities across datasets. Cybulska and Vossen (2014) and Guha et al. (2015) both stress the low ambiguity in the current datasets for the tasks of EvC and EnC.

In Ilievski et al. (2016), we measure the properties of existing disambiguation datasets for the tasks of EL, WSD, EvC, EnC, and Semantic Role Labeling (SRL), through a set of generic representation metrics applicable over tasks. The analyzed datasets show a notable bias with respect to aspects of ambiguity, variance, dominance, and time, thus exposing a strong semantic overfitting to a very limited, and within that, popular part of the world.

The problem of overfitting to a limited set of test data has been addressed by the field of domain adaptation (Daume III, 2007; Carpuat et al., 2013; Jiang and Zhai, 2007). In addition, unsupervised domain-adversarial approaches attempt to build systems that generalize beyond the specifics of a given dataset, e.g. by favoring features that apply to both the source and target domains (Ganin et al., 2016). By evaluating on another domain than the training one, these efforts have provided valuable insights into system performance. Nevertheless, this research has not addressed the aspects of time and location. Moreover, to our knowledge, no approach has been proposed to generalize the problem of reference to unseen domains, which may be due to the enormous amount of references that exist in the world leading to an almost infinite amount of possible classes.

### 2.2 The Long Tail in QA tasks

The sentence selection datasets WikiQA (Yang et al., 2015) and QASent (Wang et al., 2007) consist of questions that are collected from validated user query logs, while the answers are annotated manually from automatically selected Wikipedia pages. WIKIREADING (Hewlett et al., 2016) is a recent large-scale dataset that is based on the structured information from Wikidata (Vrandečić and Krötzsch, 2014) and the unstructured information from Wikipedia. Following a smart fully-automated data acquisition strategy, this dataset contains questions about 884 properties of 4.7 million instances. While these datasets require semantic text processing of the questions and the candidate answers, there is a finite set of answers, many of which represent popular interpretations from the world, as a direct consequence of using Wikipedia. To our knowledge, no QA task has been created to deliberately address the problem of (co)reference to long tail instances, where the list of potential interpretations is enormous, largely ambiguous, and only relevant within a specific context. The long tail aspect could be emphasized by an event-driven QA task, since the referential ambiguity of events in the world is much higher than the ambiguity of entities. No event-driven QA task has been proposed in past work. As Wikipedia only represents a tiny and popular subset of all world events, the Wikipedia-based approaches could not be applied to create such a task, thus signaling the need for a novel data acquisition approach to create an event-driven QA task for the long tail.

Weston et al. (2015) propose 20 skill sets for a comprehensive QA system. This work presents reasoning categories (e.g. spatial and temporal reasoning) and requires within-document coreference, which are very relevant skills for understanding linguistic phenomena of the long tail. However, the answer in these tasks is usually mentioned in the text, thus not addressing the referential complexity of the long tail phenomena in the world.

## 3 Moving away from semantic overfitting

Current datasets only cover a small portion of the full complexity of the disambiguation task, focusing mostly on the head. This has encouraged systems to overfit on the head and largely ignore the linguistic tail. Due to this lack of representativeness, we are not able to determine to which degree systems achieve language understanding of the long tail.

As described in the previous Section, the challenge of semantic overfitting has been recognized by past work. QA datasets, such as WIKIREADING, have increased the complexity of interpretation by using a large number of entities and questions, also allowing for subsets to be sampled to tackle specific tasks. The skill sets presented by Weston et al. (2015) include long tail skills that are crucial in order to interpret language in various micro-contexts. None of these approaches has yet created a task that addresses the long tail explicitly and recognizes the full referential complexity of disambiguation. Considering the competitiveness of the field, such task is necessary to motivate systems that can deal with the long tail and adapt to new contexts.

We therefore advocate a task that requires a deep semantic processing linked to both the head and the long tail. It is time to create a high-level referential challenge for semantic NLP that reflects a higher degree of ambiguity and variation and captures a wide range of small real-world phenomena. This task can not be solved by only capturing the head phenomena of the disambiguation tasks in any sample text collection. For maximum complexity, we propose an event-driven QA task that also represents local events, thus capturing phenomena from both the head and the long tail. Also, these events should be described across multiple documents that exhibit a natural topical spread over time, providing information bit-by-bit as it becomes available.

## 4 Task requirements

We define five requirements that should be satisfied by an event-driven QA task in order to maximize confusability, to challenge systems to deal with the tail of the Zipfian distribution, and to adapt to new contexts. These requirements apply to a single event topic, e.g. *murder*. Each event topic should contain:

**R1** Multiple event instances per event topic, e.g. *the murder of John Doe* and *the murder of Jane Roe*.

**R2** Multiple event mentions per event instance within the same document.

**R3** Multiple documents with varying document creation times in which the same event instances are described to capture topical information over time.

**R4** Event confusability by combining one or multiple confusion factors:

a) ambiguity of event surface forms, e.g. *John Smith fires a gun*, and *John Smith fires an employee*.

b) variance of event surface forms, e.g. *John Smith kills John Doe*, and *John Smith murders John Doe*.

c) time, e.g. *murder A that happened in January 1993*, and *murder B in October 2014*.

d) participants, e.g. *murder A committed by John Doe*, and *murder B committed by the Roe couple*.

e) location, e.g. *murder A that happened in Oklahoma*, and *murder B in Zaire*.

**R5** Representation of non-dominant events and entities, i.e. instances that receive little media coverage. Hence, the entities would not be restricted to celebrities and the events not to general elections.

## 5 Proposal

We propose a semantic task that represents the linguistic long tail. The task will consist of one high-level challenge (QA), for which an understanding of the long tail of several disambiguation tasks (EL, WSD, EvC, EnC) is needed in order to perform well on the high-level challenge. The QA task would feature two levels of event-oriented questions: instance-level questions (e.g. *Who was killed last summer in Vienna?*) and aggregation-level questions (e.g. *How many white people have been poisoned in the last 2 years?*). The setup would be such that the QA challenge could in theory be addressed without performing any disambiguation (e.g. using enhanced Information Retrieval), but deeper processing, especially on the disambiguation tasks, would be almost necessary in practice to be able to come up with the correct answers.

To some extent, the requirements in Section 4 are satisfied by an existing corpus, ECB+ (Cybulska and Vossen, 2014), which contains 43 event topics. For each event topic in the corpus, there are at least 2 different seminal events (R1). Since the corpus contains 7,671 intra-document coreference links, on average 7.8 per document, we can assume that requirement R2 is satisfied to a large extent. Although there are multiple news articles per event instance, they are not spread over time, which means that R3 is not satisfied. Furthermore, the event confusability factors (R4) are not fully represented, since the ambiguity and variance of the event surface forms and the participants are still very low, whereas the dominance is quite standard (R5), which is not surprising given that these aspects were not considered during the corpus assembly period. Additionally, only 1.8 sentences per document were annotated on average. Potential references in the remaining sentences need to be validated as well.

We will start with the ECB+ corpus and expand it by following an event topic-based strategy:[3]

1) Pick a subset of ECB+ topics, by favoring: a) seminal events (e.g. *murder*) whose surface forms have a low lexical ambiguity, but can be referred to by many different surface forms (*execute, slay, kill*) b) combinations of two or more seminal events that can be referred to by the same polysemous form (e.g. *firing*).

2) Select one or more confusability factors from R4, e.g. by choosing *participants* and *variance*. This step can be repeated for different combinations of the confusability factors.

3) Increase the amount of events for an event topic (to satisfy R1). We add new events based on the confusability factors chosen in step 2 and from local news sources to ensure low dominance (R5). These events can come from different documents or the same document.

4) Retrieve multiple event mentions for each event based on the decision from the confusability factors (R4). We use local news sources to ensure low dominance (R5). They originate from the same document (R2) and from different documents with (slightly) different creation times (R3).

In order to facilitate the expansion described in steps 3 and 4, we will add documents to ECB+ from The Signal Media One-Million News Articles Dataset (Signal1M) (Corney et al., 2016). This will assist in satisfying requirement R5, since the Signal1M Dataset is a collection of mostly local news. For the expansion, active learning will be applied on the Signal1M Dataset, guided by the decisions in step 2, to decide which event mentions are coreferential and which are not. By following our four-step acquisition strategy and by using the active learning method, we expect to obtain a high accuracy on EvC. As we do not expect perfect accuracy of EvC even within this smart acquisition, we will validate the active learning output. The validation will lead to a reliable set of events on a semantic level for which we would be able to pose both instance-level and aggregation-level questions, as anticipated earlier in this Section. As the task of QA does not require full annotation of all disambiguation tasks, we would be able to avoid excessive annotation work.

## 6 Conclusions

This paper addressed the issue of semantic overfitting to disambiguation datasets. Existing disambiguation datasets expose lack of representativeness and bias towards the head interpretation, while largely ignoring the rich set of long tail phenomena. Systems are discouraged to consider the full complexity of the disambiguation task, since the main incentive lies in modelling the head phenomena. To address this issue, we defined a set of requirements that should be satisfied by a semantic task in order to inspire systems that can deal with the linguistic tail and adapt to new contexts. Based on these requirements, we proposed a high-level task, QA, that requires a deep understanding of each disambiguation task in order to perform well.

[3]The same procedure can be followed for an entity-centric expansion approach.

## References


[Carpuat et al.2013] Marine Carpuat, Hal Daumé III, Katharine Henry, Ann Irvine, Jagadeesh Jagarlamudi, and Rachel Rudinger. 2013. Sensespotting: Never let your parallel data tie you to an old domain. In *Proceedings of the Association for Computational Linguistics (ACL)*. Citeseer.

[Corney et al.2016] David Corney, Dyaa Albakour, Miguel Martinez, and Samir Moussa. 2016. What do a million news articles look like? In *Proceedings of the First International Workshop on Recent Trends in News Information Retrieval co-located with 38th European Conference on Information Retrieval (ECIR 2016), Padua, Italy, March 20, 2016.*, pages 42–47.

[Cybulska and Vossen2014] Agata Cybulska and Piek Vossen. 2014. Using a sledgehammer to crack a nut? lexical diversity and event coreference resolution. In *Proceedings of the International Conference on Language Resources and Evaluation (LREC)*, pages 4545–4552.

[Daume III2007] Hal Daume III. 2007. Frustratingly easy domain adaptation. In *Proceedings of the 45th Annual Meeting of the Association of Computational Linguistics (ACL 2007)*, pages 256–263, Prague, Czech Republic. Association for Computational Linguistics.

[Ganin et al.2016] Yaroslav Ganin, Evgeniya Ustinova, Hana Ajakan, Pascal Germain, Hugo Larochelle, François Laviolette, Mario Marchand, and Victor Lempitsky. 2016. Domain-adversarial training of neural networks. *Journal of Machine Learning Research*, 17(59):1–35.

[Guha et al.2015] Anupam Guha, Mohit Iyyer, Danny Bouman, Jordan Boyd-Graber, and Jordan Boyd. 2015. Removing the training wheels: A coreference dataset that entertains humans and challenges computers. In *North American Association for Computational Linguistics (NAACL)*.

[Hewlett et al.2016] Daniel Hewlett, Alexandre Lacoste, Llion Jones, Illia Polosukhin, Andrew Fandrianto, Jay Han, Matthew Kelcey, and David Berthelot. 2016. Wikireading: A novel large-scale language understanding task over wikipedia. In *Proceedings of the 54th Annual Meeting of the Association for Computational Linguistics (Volume 1: Long Papers)*, pages 1535–1545. Association for Computational Linguistics.

[Ilievski et al.2016] Filip Ilievski, Marten Postma, and Piek Vossen. 2016. Semantic overfitting: what 'world' do we consider when evaluating disambiguation of text? *In proceedings of COLING.*

[Jiang and Zhai2007] Jing Jiang and ChengXiang Zhai. 2007. Instance weighting for domain adaptation in NLP. In *Proceedings of the 45th Annual Meeting of the Association of Computational Linguistics (ACL 2007)*, volume 7, pages 264–271.

[Newman2005] Mark EJ Newman. 2005. Power laws, pareto distributions and zipf's law. *Contemporary physics*, 46(5):323–351.

[Page et al.1999] Lawrence Page, Sergey Brin, Rajeev Motwani, and Terry Winograd. 1999. The PageRank citation ranking: bringing order to the web.

[Preiss2006] Judita Preiss. 2006. A detailed comparison of WSD systems: an analysis of the system answers for the Senseval-2 English all words task. *Natural Language Engineering*, 12(03):209–228.

[van Erp et al.2016] Marieke van Erp, Pablo Mendes, Heiko Paulheim, Filip Ilievski, Julien Plu, Giuseppe Rizzo, and Jorg Waiterlonis. 2016. Evaluating entity linking: An analysis of current benchmark datasets and a roadmap for doing a better job. In *Proceedings of the International Conference on Language Resources and Evaluation (LREC)*.

[Vossen et al.2013] Piek Vossen, Ruben Izquierdo, and Atilla Görög. 2013. DutchSemCor: in quest of the ideal sense-tagged corpus. In *Proceedings of Recent Advances in Natural Language Processing (RANLP)*, pages 710–718. INCOMA Ltd. Shoumen, Bulgaria.

[Vrandečić and Krötzsch2014] Denny Vrandečić and Markus Krötzsch. 2014. Wikidata: a free collaborative knowledgebase. *Communications of the ACM*, 57(10):78–85.

[Wang et al.2007] Mengqiu Wang, Noah A Smith, and Teruko Mitamura. 2007. What is the jeopardy model? a quasi-synchronous grammar for qa. In *EMNLP-CoNLL*, volume 7, pages 22–32.

[Weston et al.2015] Jason Weston, Antoine Bordes, Sumit Chopra, Alexander M Rush, Bart van Merriënboer, Armand Joulin, and Tomas Mikolov. 2015. Towards ai-complete question answering: A set of prerequisite toy tasks. *arXiv preprint arXiv:1502.05698.*

[Yang et al.2015] Yi Yang, Wen-tau Yih, and Christopher Meek. 2015. Wikiqa: A challenge dataset for open-domain question answering. In *Proceedings of EMNLP*, pages 2013–2018. Citeseer.

# Unsupervised Event Coreference for Abstract Words

**Dheeraj Rajagopal** and **Eduard Hovy** and **Teruko Mitamura**
Language Technologies Institute
Carnegie Mellon University
dheeraj@cs.cmu.edu, hovy@cmu.edu, teruko@cs.cmu.edu

## Abstract

We introduce a novel approach for resolving coreference when the trigger word refers to multiple (sometimes non-contiguous) clauses. Our approach is completely unsupervised, and our experiments show that Neural Network models perform much better (about 20% more accurate) than traditional feature-rich baseline models. We also present a new dataset for Biomedical Language Processing which, with only about 25% of the original corpus vocabulary, still captures the essential distributional semantics of the corpus.

## 1 Introduction

Event coreference is a key module in many NLP applications, especially those that involve multisentence discourse. Current event coreference systems restrict the problem to finding a correspondence between trigger words or phrases and their fully coreferent event (word or phrase). This approach is rather limited since it does not handle the case when the trigger refers to several events as a group, as in

> We worked hard all our lives. But one year we **went on vacation. There was boating, crazy adventure sports, and pro-golfing. We also spent time in the evenings strolling around the park**. But eventually we had to go home. There couldn't have been a better **vacation**.

In this paper we generalize the idea of coreference to 3 levels based on the degree of abstraction of the coreference trigger:

1. Level 1 – Direct Mention: The trigger phrase is specific and usually matches the referring event(s) word-for-word or phrase-for-phrase.

2. Level 2 – Single Clause: While there is a similar word-to-phrase or word-to-word relationship as in level 1, the trigger is a more generic event compared to level 1.

3. Level 3 – Multiple Clauses: The trigger is quite generic and refers to a particular instance of an event that is described over multiple clauses or sentences (either contiguous or non-contiguous). Typically, the abstract event refers to a set of [sub]events, each of them with its own own participants or arguments.

See Table 1 for examples.

We use PubMed[1] as our primary corpus.

Almost all work on event coreference (for example, (Liu et al., 2014) (Lee et al., 2012)) applies to levels 1 or 2. In this paper, we propose a generalized coreference classification scheme and address the challenges related to resolving level-3 coreferences.

Creating gold-standard training and evaluation materials for such coreferences is an uphill challenge. First, there is a significant annotation overhead and, depending on the nature of the corpus, the annotator might require significant domain knowledge. Each annotation instance might require multiple labels depending the number of abstract events mentioned in the corpus. Second, the vocabulary of the corpus is rather large due to domain-related

[1] http://www.ncbi.nlm.nih.gov/pmc/tools/openftlist/



*Proceedings of EMNLP 2016 Workshop on Uphill Battles in Language Processing: Scaling Early Achievements to Robust Methods*, pages 22–26,
Austin, TX, November 5, 2016. ©2016 Association for Computational Linguistics

| | |
|---|---|
| level 1 | In turn the activated **ERK phosphorylates Stim1 at serine 575**, and **this phosphorylation** enhances complex formation of Stim1 |
| level 2 | (a) **BMI1 enhances hTERT activity**. (b) **This effect** was attenuated by PTEN , PTEN ( CS ) , PTEN ( GE ) , and C-PTEN. |
| level 3 | (a) **To determine whether these clumps were also associated with the cell cortex, we used confocal microscopy.** (b) **The actin clumps were found associated with the cell cortex in only a minority of cases ( Fig . 4 ).** (c) Immuno-EM using anti-actin antibodies has verified **this observation** |

**Table 1:** Examples of various levels of Coreference (triggers are underlined and referent indicated in bold)

named entities like proteins, cell-types, DNA and RNA names. The large vocabulary size necessitates longer and sparser vectors for representing the documents, resulting in significant data sparsity. Last, evaluating such a system in an unsupervised setting usually leads to debatable justifications for evaluating the models. We address these challenges in the following ways:

1. We construct a new dataset, derived from the PubMed corpus, by replacing all named entities with their respective NE label. We normalize Proteins, Cell lines, Cell types, RNA and DNA names using the tagger described in (Tsuruoka et al., 2005). Also, we normalize all *figure* and *table* references to "internal_link", and citations to other studies as "external_link". This significantly reduces the vocabulary of the dataset.

2. We present an unsupervised model to represent abstract coreferences in text. We present multiple baseline systems using the traditional *Bag-of-Words* model and a Neural Network architecture that outperforms the baseline models.

3. We define a cloze-test evaluation method that requires no annotation. Our procedure stems from the following insight. Instead of starting with the coreference trigger word/phrase and asking "which clauses can refer to this?", we train an algorithm to *predict* for a given clause which trigger word/phrase it would 'prefer to' link to, and then apply this algorithm to [sequences of] clauses within the likely scope of reference of a trigger. An example is shown in Table 2. A similar idea was mentioned in (Hermann et al., 2015).

| |
|---|
| *Passage :* BAF57 has been shown to directly interact with the androgen and estrogen receptors. We used co-immunoprecipitation experiments to test whether BAF57 forms a complex with PR in cultured cells. In the absence of hormone, a certain proportion of BAF57 already coprecipitated with PR probably due to the large proportion of PR molecules already present in the nucleus in the uninduced state; however 30 minutes after hormone addition the extent of coprecipitation was increased. In contrast, no complex of PR with the PBAF specific subunit, BAF180 was observed independently of the addition of the hormone. As a positive control for *ABSTRACT_COREF_EVENT* we used BAF250, a known BAF specific subunit. |
| *Task*: Predict *ABSTRACT_COREF_EVENT* from the list of all abstract events of interest |
| *Answer*: this experiment |

**Table 2:** A sample cloze-test evaluation task

## 2 Related Work

Entity coreference has been studied quite extensively. There are primarily two complementary approaches. The first focuses mainly on identifying entity mention clusters (see (Haghighi and Klein, 2009), (Raghunathan et al., 2010), (Ponzetto and Strube, 2006), (Rahman and Ng, 2011), (Ponzetto and Strube, 2006)). These models employ feature-rich approaches to improve the clustering models and are limited to noun pairs. The second focuses on jointly modeling mentions across all the entries in the document (see (Denis et al., 2007), (Poon and Domingos, 2008), (Wick et al., 2008) and (Lee et al., 2011)). Some more recent work uses event argument information to assist entity coreference; this includes (Rahman and Ng, 2011), (Haghighi and

Klein, 2010).

The distinct problem of Event Coreference has been relatively underexplored. Some earlier work in this area includes (Humphreys et al., 1997) but the work was very specific to selected events. More recently, there have been approaches to model event coreferences separately (Liu et al., 2014) as well as jointly with entities (Lee et al., 2012). All this work makes the limiting assumption of word/phrase to word/phrase coreference (levels 1 and 2 described earlier). Our work aligns with the event coreference literature but assumes longer spans of text and tackles the more challenging problem of abstract multi-event/clause coreference.

## 3 Model

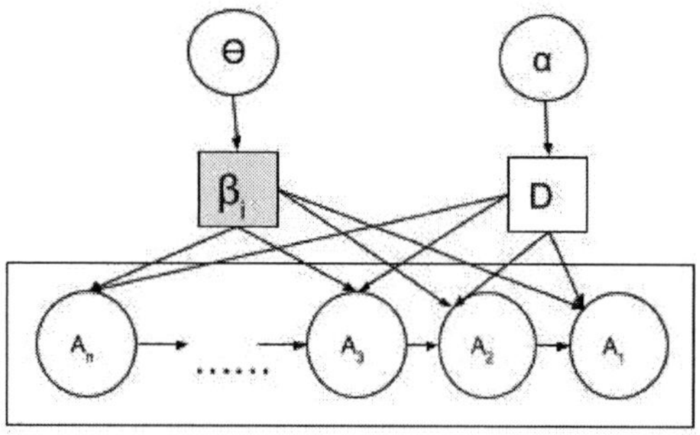


**Figure 1:** Architecture Diagram for the Coreference Model

Let $\beta_i$ be the coreference word/phrase generated from a distribution parameterized by $\theta$. Each $\beta_i$ generates antecedents $A_{1..n}$ (sentences that lead towards the coreference) that contain the coreferent span. These antecendents also obey a dependency relationship between two adjacent sentences in discourse. Since multi-clause coreference shows a distinct effect of recency, we also define a decay function $D$ parameterized by $\alpha$. The decay function $D$ dictates how the level of association of each antecendent varies over increasing sentence distance.

### 3.1 Distributed Representation of Sentences

To simplify modeling complexity, we first ensure that all the antecedents are represented by vectors of the same dimension. We use the sentence2vec representation from (Le and Mikolov, 2014) to generate a 300-dimensional continuous distributed representation for each sentence in the PubMed corpus. These vectors are trained using gradient descent, with gradients are obtained though back-propagation. This allows us to reduce the parameters that would have been necessary to model the number of words in each sentence. Table 3 shows some example events and their preferred coreference trigger.

| | |
|---|---|
| phosphorylation | phophorylation, phospory-lation, phoshorylation, dephosphorylation, phos-phorylations, Phospho-rylation, autophosphory-lation, phosphorilation, auto-phosphorylation, phos-phorylated |
| ubiquitination | ubiquitylation, ubiquitiny-lation, polyubiquitination, poly-ubiquitination, SUMOy-lation, polyubiquitylation, deubiquitination, sumoy-lation, autoubiquitination, mono-ubiquitination |
| concluded | speculated, hypothesized, hy-pothesised, argued, surmised, conclude, postulated, noticed, noted, postulate |

**Table 3:** Top trigger words (left) under Word2Vec similarity for sample events (right)

### 3.2 Multilayer Perceptron Model

The MultiLayer Perceptron (MLP) model is given by the function $f : R^D \rightarrow R^L$, where D is the size of input vector x and L is the size of the output vector f(x),

$$f(x) = G\left(b^{(2)} + W^{(2)}\left(s\left(b^{(1)} + W^{(1)}x\right)\right)\right) \quad (1)$$

with bias vectors $b^{(1)}$ , $b^{(2)}$ ; weight matrices $W^{(1)}$, $W^{(2)}$ and activation functions G (softmax) and s (tanh).

For our model, the input dimensions are 300-dimensional sentence vectors. We define 6 classes (6 distinct trigger words) for output. The antecedents are represented using a single vector, composed from the $N$ chosen input clauses, where we vary $N$ from 1 ato 5. For composition we currently use simple average. We assume no decay currently. The architecture diagram is shown in Figure 2.

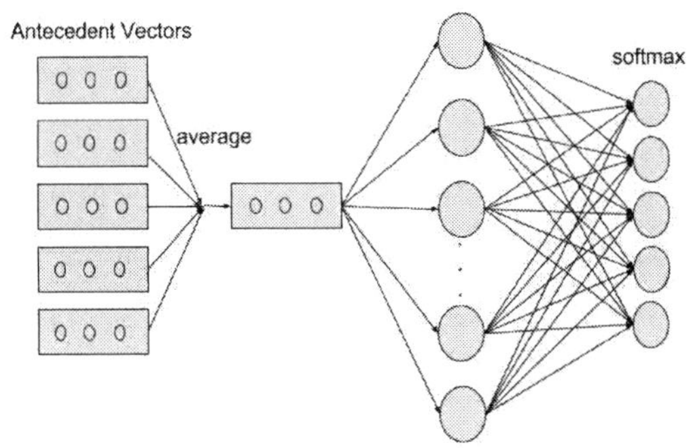


**Figure 2:** Architecture Diagram for MLP

| Classifier | Accuracy |
|---|---|
| Linear SVM | 0.436 |
| SGD Classifer | 0.39 |
| BernoulliNB | 0.349 |
| Random Forest | 0.34 |
| AdaBoost | 0.359 |
| DecisionTree | 0.286 |
| **MLP** | **0.62** |

**Table 4:** Results for various baselines and our work

## 4 Experiments

The Cloze-test evaluation is inspired by the reading comprehension evaluation from Question-Answering research. In this evaluation, the system first reads a passage and then attempts to predict missing words from sentences that contain information from the passage. For our evaluation, we use a slightly modified version of the Cloze-test, in which the model is trained for each coreference with sentences that appear before and after the coreference. Currently, we arbitrarily limit the number of sentences in the antecedent and precedent span for coreference to 5. Also, we consider only 6 labels for now, namely *these changes, these responses, this analysis, this context,this finding, this observation.*

### 4.1 Experimental Setup

In order to maintain the even distribution of coreference candidates, we derived our dataset from the PubMed corpus by selecting 1000 samples of each of the 6 coreferent labels for a total of 6000 training samples, each sample containing the coreference trigger and we pick antecedent sentences based on the following criteria. If the coreference occurs in the same paragraph, the number of antecedent sentences are limited to sentences from the start of the paragraph or upto five antecedent sentence candidates otherwise. For the MLP model, we use a 70-30 train-test split and apply the early stopping criteria based on accuracy drop on the validation dataset.

### 4.2 Results

Our results show that our MLP model outperforms all other feature-rich baseline models of traditional classifiers. Although there is general skepticism around sentence vectors, our experiments show that RNN and LSTM models are suitable for the generalized coreference task.

Although we train using a window of $N$ clauses together, during run-time we obtain the prediction for individual sentences rather than taking the average over a window. The label of each sentence or clause depends on the preference of its immediate neighbours, and how these sentences form a 'span', to arrive at a general 'consensus' label. This testing criteria can be further improved by using advanced similarity and coherence detection methods. For now, if the predicted class for that particular sentence is the same as the true label, then that sentence is labeled as part of the coreference.

## 5 Conclusion and Future Work

We presented a classification taxonomy that generalizes types of event coreference. We presented a model for unsupervised abstract coreference. We described a new dataset for biomedical text that is suitable for any generalized biomedical NLP task. Our Cloze-test evaluation method makes annotation unnecessary.

Since this one of the first works to explore abstract event coreference, there is an uphill task of developing more principled approaches towards modeling and evaluation. We also plan to explore more sophisticated models for our architecture and get more insights into sentence vectors. Also, we plan to extend this idea of coreference into other data domains like News corpus and probably extend to entity-coreference work as well.

## Acknowledgments

This research was supported in part by U.S. Army Research Office (ARO) grant W911NF-14-1-0436 under DARPA's Big Mechanisms Program. Any opinion, findings, and conclusions or recommendations expressed in this material are those of the authors and do not necessarily reflect the view of DARPA, ARO, or the U.S. government.

## References

Pascal Denis, Jason Baldridge, et al. 2007. Joint determination of anaphoricity and coreference resolution using integer programming. In *HLT-NAACL*, pages 236–243. Citeseer.

Aria Haghighi and Dan Klein. 2009. Simple coreference resolution with rich syntactic and semantic features. In *Proceedings of the 2009 Conference on Empirical Methods in Natural Language Processing: Volume 3-Volume 3*, pages 1152–1161. Association for Computational Linguistics.

Aria Haghighi and Dan Klein. 2010. Coreference resolution in a modular, entity-centered model. In *Human Language Technologies: The 2010 Annual Conference of the North American Chapter of the Association for Computational Linguistics*, pages 385–393. Association for Computational Linguistics.

Karl Moritz Hermann, Tomas Kocisky, Edward Grefenstette, Lasse Espeholt, Will Kay, Mustafa Suleyman, and Phil Blunsom. 2015. Teaching machines to read and comprehend. In *Advances in Neural Information Processing Systems*, pages 1693–1701.

Kevin Humphreys, Robert Gaizauskas, and Saliha Azzam. 1997. Event coreference for information extraction. In *Proceedings of a Workshop on Operational Factors in Practical, Robust Anaphora Resolution for Unrestricted Texts*, pages 75–81. Association for Computational Linguistics.

Quoc V Le and Tomas Mikolov. 2014. Distributed representations of sentences and documents. In *ICML*, volume 14, pages 1188–1196.

Heeyoung Lee, Yves Peirsman, Angel Chang, Nathanael Chambers, Mihai Surdeanu, and Dan Jurafsky. 2011. Stanford's multi-pass sieve coreference resolution system at the conll-2011 shared task. In *Proceedings of the Fifteenth Conference on Computational Natural Language Learning: Shared Task*, pages 28–34. Association for Computational Linguistics.

Heeyoung Lee, Marta Recasens, Angel Chang, Mihai Surdeanu, and Dan Jurafsky. 2012. Joint entity and event coreference resolution across documents. In *Proceedings of the 2012 Joint Conference on Empirical Methods in Natural Language Processing and Computational Natural Language Learning*, pages 489–500. Association for Computational Linguistics.

Zhengzhong Liu, Jun Araki, Eduard H Hovy, and Teruko Mitamura. 2014. Supervised within-document event coreference using information propagation. In *LREC*, pages 4539–4544.

Simone Paolo Ponzetto and Michael Strube. 2006. Exploiting semantic role labeling, wordnet and wikipedia for coreference resolution. In *Proceedings of the main conference on Human Language Technology Conference of the North American Chapter of the Association of Computational Linguistics*, pages 192–199. Association for Computational Linguistics.

Hoifung Poon and Pedro Domingos. 2008. Joint unsupervised coreference resolution with markov logic. In *Proceedings of the conference on empirical methods in natural language processing*, pages 650–659. Association for Computational Linguistics.

Karthik Raghunathan, Heeyoung Lee, Sudarshan Rangarajan, Nathanael Chambers, Mihai Surdeanu, Dan Jurafsky, and Christopher Manning. 2010. A multi-pass sieve for coreference resolution. In *Proceedings of the 2010 Conference on Empirical Methods in Natural Language Processing*, pages 492–501. Association for Computational Linguistics.

Altaf Rahman and Vincent Ng. 2011. Coreference resolution with world knowledge. In *Proceedings of the 49th Annual Meeting of the Association for Computational Linguistics: Human Language Technologies-Volume 1*, pages 814–824. Association for Computational Linguistics.

Yoshimasa Tsuruoka, Yuka Tateishi, Jin-Dong Kim, Tomoko Ohta, John McNaught, Sophia Ananiadou, and Junichi Tsujii. 2005. Developing a robust part-of-speech tagger for biomedical text. In *Panhellenic Conference on Informatics*, pages 382–392. Springer.

Michael L Wick, Khashayar Rohanimanesh, Karl Schultz, and Andrew McCallum. 2008. A unified approach for schema matching, coreference and canonicalization. In *Proceedings of the 14th ACM SIGKDD international conference on Knowledge discovery and data mining*, pages 722–730. ACM.

# Towards Broad-coverage Meaning Representation: The Case of Comparison Structures

**Omid Bakhshandeh**
University of Rochester
omidb@cs.rochester.edu

**James F. Allen**
University of Rochester / IHMC
james@cs.rochester.edu

## 1 Introduction

Representing the underlying meaning of text has been a long-standing topic of interest in computational linguistics. Recently there has been a renewed interest in computational modeling of meaning for various tasks such as semantic parsing (Zelle and Mooney, 1996; Berant and Liang, 2014). Open-domain and broad-coverage semantic representation (Banarescu et al., 2013; Bos, 2008; Allen et al., 2008) is essential for many language understanding tasks such as reading comprehension tests and question answering.

One of the most common way for expressing evaluative sentiment towards different entities is to use comparison. Comparison can happen in very simple structures such as *'John is taller than Susan'*, or more complicated constructions such as *'The table is longer than the sofa is wide'*. So far the computational semantics of comparatives and how they affect the meaning of the surrounding text has not been studied effectively. That is, the difference between the existing semantic and syntactic representation of comparatives has not been distinctive enough for enabling deeper understanding of a sentence. For instance, the general logical form representation of the sentence *'John is taller than Susan'* using the Boxer system (Bos, 2008) is the following:

$$named(x0, john, per) \\ \& \; named(x1, susan, nam) \\ \& than(taller(x0), x1) \quad (1)$$

Clearly, the above meaning representation does not fully capture the underlying semantics of the adjective 'tall' and what it means to be 'taller'. A human reader can easily infer that the 'height' attribute of John is greater than Susan's. Capturing the underlying meaning of comparison structures, as opposed to their surface wording, is crucial for accurate evaluation of qualities and quantities. Consider a more complex comparison example, *'The pizza was great, but it was still worse than the sandwich'*. The state-of-the-art sentiment analysis system (Manning et al., 2014) assigns an overall 'negative' sentiment value to this sentence, which clearly lacks the understanding of the comparison happening in the sentence.

| My Mazda | drove | faster than his Hyundai |
|---|---|---|
| Self_mover | **Self_motion** | Manner |

Figure 1: The frame-semantic parsing of the sentence *My Mazda drove faster than his Hyundai.*

As another example, consider the generic meaning representation of the sentence *'My Mazda drove faster than his Hyundai'*, according to frame semantic parsing using Semafor[1] tool (Das et al., 2014) as depicted in Figure 1. It is evident that this meaning representation does not fully capture how the semantics of the adjective *fast* relates to the *driving* event, and what it actually means for a car to drive *faster than* another car. More importantly, there is an ellipsis in this sentence, the resolution of which results in complete reading of *'My Mazda drove faster than his Hyundai drove fast'*, which is in no way captured in Figure 1[2].

[1] http://demo.ark.cs.cmu.edu/parse

[2] The same shortcomings are shared among other generic meaning representations such as LinGO English Resource



*Proceedings of EMNLP 2016 Workshop on Uphill Battles in Language Processing: Scaling Early Achievements to Robust Methods*, pages 27–31, Austin, TX, November 5, 2016. 

Although the syntax and semantics of comparison in language have been studied in linguistics for a long time (Bresnan, 1973; Cresswell, 1976; Von Stechow, 1984), so far, computational modeling of the semantics of comparison components of natural language has not been developed fundamentally. The lack of such a computational framework has left the deeper understanding of comparison structures still baffling to the currently existing NLP systems. In this paper we summarize our efforts on defining a joint framework for comprehensive semantic representation of the comparison and ellipsis constructions. We jointly model comparison and ellipsis as inter-connected predicate-argument structures, which enables automatic ellipsis resolution. In the upcoming sections we summarize our main contributions to this topic.

## 2 A Comprehensive Semantic Framework for Comparison and Ellipsis

We introduce a novel framework for modeling the semantics of comparison and ellipsis as inter-connected predicate-argument structures. According to this framework, comparison and ellipsis operators are the predicates, where each predicate has a set of arguments called its *semantic frame*. For example, in the sentence *'[Sam] is the tallest [student] [in the gym]'*, the morpheme *-est* is the comparison operator (hence, the comparison predicate) and the entities in the brackets are the arguments.

### 2.1 Comparison Structures

#### 2.1.1 Predicates

We consider two main categories of comparison predicates (Bakhshandeh and Allen, 2015; Bakhshandeh et al., 2016), Ordering and Extreme, each of which can grade any of the four parts of speech including adjectives, adverbs, nouns, and verbs.

• **Ordering**: Shows the ordering of two or more entities on a scale, with the following subtypes:

– Comparatives expressed by the morphemes *more/-er* and *less*, with '$>$', '$<$' indicating that one degree is greater or lesser than the other.

(1) The steak is tastier than the potatoes.

Grammar (ERG) (Flickinger, 2011), Boxer (Bos, 2008), or AMR (Banarescu et al., 2013), among others.

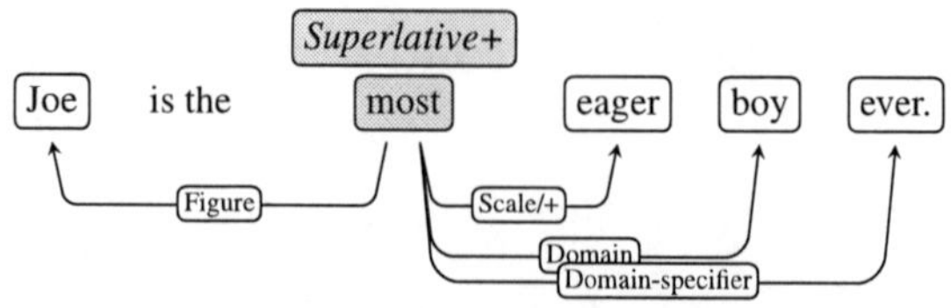


Figure 2: An example predicate-argument structure consisting of superlative predicate type and its corresponding semantic frame of arguments.

– Equatives expressed by *as* in constructions such as *as tall* or *as much*, with '$\geq$' indicating that one degree equals or is greater than another.

(2) The Mazda drives as fast as the Nissan.

– Superlatives expressed by *most/-est* and *least*, indicates that an entity or event has the 'highest' or 'lowest' degree on a scale.

(3) That chef made the best soup.

The details of the Extreme type can be found in the earlier work (Bakhshandeh and Allen, 2015; Bakhshandeh et al., 2016).

#### 2.1.2 Arguments

Each predicate takes a set of arguments that we refer to as the predicate's 'semantic frame'. Following are the main arguments included in our framework:

– Figure (Fig): The main role which is being compared.

– Ground: The main role Figure is compared to.

– Scale: The scale for the comparison, such as length, depth, speed. For a more detailed study on scales please refer to the work on learning adjective scales (Bakhshandeh and Allen, 2015).

Our framework also includes 'Standard', 'Differential', 'Domain', and 'Domain Specifier' argument types. Figure 2 shows an example meaning representations based on our framework.

### 2.2 Ellipsis Structures

As mentioned earlier in Section 1, resolving ellipsis in comparison structures is crucial for language understanding and failure to do so would deliver an incorrect meaning representation. In linguistics various subtypes of elliptical constructions are studied (Kennedy, 2003; Merchant, 2013; Yoshida et al., 2016). In our framework we mainly include six types which are seen in comparison structures (Bakhshandeh et al., 2016): ‘VP-deletion’, ‘Stripping’[3], ‘Pseudo-gapping’, ‘Gapping’, ‘Sluicing’, and ‘Subdeletion’. Ellipsis more often occurs in comparative and equative comparison constructions. A few examples of ellipsis in comparative constructions are as follows:

- **Comparatives**: Ellipsis site is the dependent clause headed by *than*. Three ellipsis possibilities for these clauses resuming (4) are shown below. The elided materials are written in subscript.

(4) **Mary drank more tea** ...

- VP-deletion (aka ‘Comparative Deletion’):
  ... than John did $_{\text{drink coffee}}$.
- Stripping (aka ‘Phrasal Comparative’):
  ... than John $_{\text{drank coffee}}$.
- Gapping:
  ... than John, $_{\text{drank } \textit{how-much}}$ coffee.
- Pseudogapping:
  ... than John did $_{\text{drank}}$ coffee.

Furthermore, we define three argument types for ellipsis, which help thoroughly construct the antecedent of the elided material by taking into account the existing words of the context sentence: Reference, Exclude, and How-much.

## 3 Data Collection Methodology

Given the new semantic representation, we aim at annotating corpora which then enables developing and testing models. The diversity and comprehensiveness of the comparison structures represented in our dataset is dependent on the genre of sentences comprising it. Earlier, we had experimented with annotating semantic structures on OntoNotes dataset (Bakhshandeh and Allen, 2015). Recently (Bakhshandeh et al., 2016), We have shifted our focus to actual product and restaurant reviews, which include many natural comparison instances. For this purpose we mainly use Google English Web Treebank[4] which comes with gold constituency parse trees. We augment this dataset with the Movie Reviews dataset (Pang and Lee, 2005), where we use Berkeley parser (Petrov et al., 2006) to obtain parse trees.

We trained linguists by asking them to read the semantic framework annotation manual as summarized in Section 2. The annotations were done via our interactive two-stage tree-based annotation tool. For this task, the annotations were done on top of constituency parse trees. This process yielded a total of 2,800 annotated sentences. Figure 3 visualizes the distribution of predicate types from the various resources. As this Figure shows, reviews are indeed a very rich resource for comparisons, having more comparison instances than any other resource of even a bigger size. There are a total of 5,564 comparison arguments in our dataset, with ‘scale’ and ‘figure’ being the majority types. The total number of ellipsis predicates is 240, with 197 Stripping, 31 VP-deletion and 12 Pseudo-gapping.

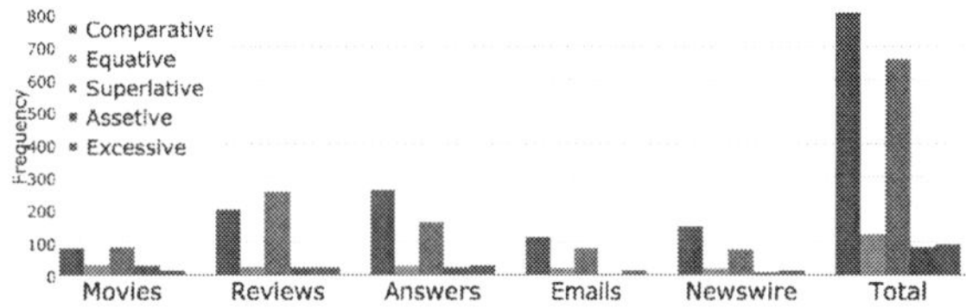


Figure 3: The number of various predicate types across different resources.

| | P | ILP Model R | F1 |
|---|---|---|---|
| Average | 0.72/0.78 | 0.91/0.97 | 0.76/0.80 |
| | | **Baseline** | |
| Average | 0.62/0.64 | 0.87/0.97 | 0.66/0.69 |

Table 1: Predicate prediction Precision (P), Recall (R) and F1 scores on test set, averaged across all predicate types. Each cell contains scores according to Exact/Head measurement.

## 4 Predicting Semantic Structures

We model the prediction problem as a joint predicate-argument prediction of comparison and ellipsis structures. In a nutshell, we define a globally normalized model for the probability distribution of comparison and ellipsis labels over all parse tree nodes as follows:

$$p_C(c|v,T,\theta_C) \propto exp(\boldsymbol{f}_C(c,T)^T\boldsymbol{\theta}_C) \quad (2)$$

$$p_{A_c}(a_c|c,e,v,T,\theta_{a_c}) \propto exp(\boldsymbol{f}_{A_C}(c,e,T)^T\boldsymbol{\theta}_{\boldsymbol{a_c}}) \quad (3)$$

where $T$ is the underlying constituency tree, $p_C$ is the probability of assigning predicate type $c$ as the predicate type and $p_{A_c}$ is the probability of assigning the argument type $a_c$ as the argument type. In

[3]VP-deletion and stripping are the more frequent types.

[4]`https://catalog.ldc.upenn.edu/LDC2012T13`

| | ILP Model (Exact/Head) | | | ILP No Constraints (Exact/Head) | | | Baseline (Exact/Head) | | |
|---|---|---|---|---|---|---|---|---|---|
| | P | R | F1 | P | R | F1 | P | R | F1 |
| **Average** | 0.37/0.61 | 0.54/0.87 | 0.43/0.71 | 0.01/0.01 | 0.86/1.00 | 0.10/0.10 | 0.20/0.42 | 0.36/0.73 | 0.25/0.52 |

Table 2: Results of argument prediction on test set, averaged across various argument types.

each of the above equations, $f$ is the corresponding feature function. For predicates and the arguments the main features are lexical features and bigram features, among many others. $\theta_C$, $\theta_E$, $\theta_{a_c}$ is the parameters of the log-linear model. We calculate these parameters using Stochastic Gradient Descent algorithm.

For inference, we model the problem as a structured prediction task. Given the syntactic tree of a given sentence, for each node we first select the predicate type with the highest $p_C$. Then for each selected comparison predicate, we find the corresponding ellipsis predicate that has the highest $p_E$ probability. We tackle the problem of argument assignment by Integer Linear Programming (ILP), where we pose domain-specific linguistic knowledge as constraints. Any specific comparison label calls for a unique set of constraints in the ILP formulation, which ensures the validity of predictions[5]. The details of this modeling can be found in earlier work (Bakhshandeh et al., 2016).

## 5 Experimental Results

We trained our ILP model on the train-dev part of the dataset (70%), and tested on the test set (30%). Evaluation is done against the reference gold annotation, with Exact and partial (Head) credits to annotating the constituency nodes. We mainly report on two models: our comprehensive ILP model (detailed in Section 4), and a rule-based baseline. In short, the baseline encodes the same linguistically motivated ILP constraints via rules and uses a few pattern extraction methods for finding comparison morphemes.

The average results on predicate prediction (across all types) is shown in Table 1. As the results show, overall, the scores are high for predicting the predicates, what is not shown here is ellipsis predicates being the most challenging. The baseline is competitive, which shows that the linguistic patterns can capture many of the predicate types. Our model performs the poorest on $Equatives$, achieving 71%/73% F1 score, which is a complex morpheme used in various linguistic constructions. Our analysis shows that the errors are often due to inaccuracies in automatically generated parse trees[6]. As you can see in Table 2, The task of predicting arguments is a more demanding task. The baseline performs very poorly at predicting the arguments. Our comprehensive ILP model consistently outperforms the *No Constraints* model, showing the effectiveness of our linguistically motivated ILP constraints.

## 6 Conclusion

In this work we summarized our work which focuses on an aspect of language with a very rich semantics: Comparison and Ellipsis. The current tools and methodologies in the research community are not able to go beyond surface-level shallow representations for comparison and ellipsis structures. We have developed widely usable comprehensive semantic theory of linguistic content of comparison structures. Our representation is broad-coverage and domain-independent, hence, can be incorporated as a part of any broad-coverage semantic parser (Banarescu et al., 2013; Allen et al., 2008; Bos, 2008) for augmenting their meaning representation.

## Acknowledgment

We thank the anonymous reviewers for their comments. This work was supported in part by Grant W911NF-15-1-0542 with the US Defense Advanced Research Projects Agency (DARPA) and the Army Research Office (ARO).

## References

James F. Allen, Mary Swift, and Will de Beaumont. 2008. Deep semantic analysis of text. In *Proceedings*

[5]For instance, the $Superlative$ predicate type never takes any $Ground$ arguments, or the argument $Standard$ is only applicable to the excessive predicate type.

[6]For example, challenging long review sentences with informal language.

*of the 2008 Conference on Semantics in Text Processing*, STEP '08, pages 343–354, Stroudsburg, PA, USA. Association for Computational Linguistics.

Omid Bakhshandeh and James Allen. 2015. Semantic framework for comparison structures in natural language. In *Proceedings of the 2015 Conference on Empirical Methods in Natural Language Processing*, pages 993–1002, Lisbon, Portugal, September. Association for Computational Linguistics.

Omid Bakhshandeh, Alexis Cornelia Wellwood, and James Allen. 2016. Learning to jointly predict ellipsis and comparison structures. In *Proceedings of The 20th SIGNLL Conference on Computational Natural Language Learning*, pages 62–74, Berlin, Germany, August. Association for Computational Linguistics.

Laura Banarescu, Claire Bonial, Shu Cai, Madalina Georgescu, Kira Griffitt, Ulf Hermjakob, Kevin Knight, Philipp Koehn, Martha Palmer, and Nathan Schneider. 2013. Abstract meaning representation for sembanking. In *Proceedings of the 7th Linguistic Annotation Workshop and Interoperability with Discourse*, pages 178–186, Sofia, Bulgaria, August. Association for Computational Linguistics.

Jonathan Berant and Percy Liang. 2014. Semantic parsing via paraphrasing. In *Association for Computational Linguistics (ACL)*.

Johan Bos. 2008. Wide-coverage semantic analysis with boxer. In Johan Bos and Rodolfo Delmonte, editors, *Semantics in Text Processing. STEP 2008 Conference Proceedings*, Research in Computational Semantics, pages 277–286. College Publications.

Joan Bresnan. 1973. Syntax of the comparative clause construction in English. *Linguistic Inquiry*, 4(3):275–343.

Max Cresswell. 1976. The semantics of degree. *Barbara Hall Partee (ed.)*, pages 261–292.

Dipanjan Das, Desai Chen, AndrÃl' F. T. Martins, Nathan Schneider, and Noah A. Smith. 2014. Frame-semantic parsing. *Computational Linguistics*, 40:1:9–56.

Dan Flickinger. 2011. Accuracy vs. robustness in grammar engineering. In Emily M. Bender and Jennifer E. Arnold, editors, *Language from a Cognitive Perspective: Grammar, Usage and Processing*, number 201, pages 31–50. CSLI Publications, Stanford.

Christopher Kennedy. 2003. Ellipsis and syntactic representation. In Kerstin Schwabe and Susanne Winkler, editors, *The Interfaces: Deriving and Interpreting Omitted Structures*, number 61 in Linguistics Aktuell, pages 29–54. John Benjamins.

Christopher D. Manning, Mihai Surdeanu, John Bauer, Jenny Finkel, Steven J. Bethard, and David McClosky. 2014. The Stanford CoreNLP natural language processing toolkit. In *Proceedings of 52nd Annual Meeting of the Association for Computational Linguistics: System Demonstrations*, pages 55–60.

Jason Merchant. 2013. Voice and ellipsis. *Linguistic Inquiry*, 44(1):77–108.

Bo Pang and Lillian Lee. 2005. Seeing stars: Exploiting class relationships for sentiment categorization with respect to rating scales. In *Proceedings of ACL*, pages 115–124.

Slav Petrov, Leon Barrett, Romain Thibaux, and Dan Klein. 2006. Learning accurate, compact, and interpretable tree annotation. In *Proceedings of the 21st International Conference on Computational Linguistics and the 44th Annual Meeting of the Association for Computational Linguistics*, ACL-44, pages 433–440, Stroudsburg, PA, USA. Association for Computational Linguistics.

Arnim Von Stechow. 1984. Comparing semantic theories of comparison. *Journal of Semantics*, 3(1):1–77.

Masaya Yoshida, Chizuru Nakao, and IvÃąn Ortega-Santos. 2016. *Ellipsis*. Routledge Handbook of Syntax, London, UK.

John M. Zelle and Raymond J. Mooney. 1996. Learning to parse database queries using inductive logic programming. In *Proceedings of the Thirteenth National Conference on Artificial Intelligence - Volume 2*, AAAI'96, pages 1050–1055. AAAI Press.

# DialPort: A General Framework for Aggregating Dialog Systems

**Tiancheng Zhao** and **Maxine Eskenazi**
Language Technologies Institute
Carnegie Mellon University
{tianchez,max+}@cs.cmu.edu

**Kyusong Lee**
Pohang University of
Science and Technology
kyusonglee@postech.ac.kr

## Abstract

This paper describes a new spoken dialog portal that connects systems produced by the spoken dialog research community and gives them access to real users. We introduce a prototype dialog framework that affords easy integration with various remote dialog agents as well as external knowledge resources. To date, the DialPort portal has successfully connected to two dialog systems and several public knowledge APIs. We present current progress and envision our future plan.

## 1 Introduction

Much fundamental research in the spoken dialog domain remains to be done, including adaption for user modeling and management of complex dialogs. In recent years, there has been increasing interest in applying deep learning to modeling the process of human-computer conversation (Vinyals and Le, 2015; Serban et al., 2015; Wen et al., 2016; Williams and Zweig, 2016; Zhao and Eskenazi, 2016). One of the prerequisites for the success of these methods is having a large conversation corpus to train on. In order to advance the research in these uphill areas of study with the state-of-the-art data-driven methods, large corpora of multi-type real user dialogs are needed. At present, few existing large corpora cover a wide set of research domains. It is also extremely difficult for any one group to devote time to collecting and curating a significant amount of real user data. The users must be found and kept interested, and the interface must be created and maintained.

Our proposed solution is DialPort, a data gathering portal that groups various types of dialog systems, gives potential users a variety of interesting applications, and shares the collected data amongst all participating research groups. The connected dialog systems are not simply listed on a website. They are fully integrated into a single virtual agent. From the user's perspective, DialPort is a dialog system that can provide information in many domains and it becomes increasingly more attractive as new research groups join and resulting more functionalities to discover.

## 2 Challenges

Besides creating new corpora for advanced dialog research, DialPort encounters new research challenges.

- *Advanced Dialog State Representation Learning*: Traditional dialog states are represented as sets of symbolic variables that are related to domain-specific ontology and are tracked by statistical methods (Williams et al., 2013). Such an approach soon becomes intractable if we want to capture all the essential dialog state features within nested multi-domain conversations, such as modeling user preferences and tracking discourse features. DialPort must address this challenge if it is to effectively serve as a portal to many systems.

- *Dialog Policy that Combines Various Types of Agents*: DialPort is powered by multiple dialog agents from research labs around the world. It is different from the traditional sin-



*Proceedings of EMNLP 2016 Workshop on Uphill Battles in Language Processing: Scaling Early Achievements to Robust Methods*, pages 32–34,
Austin, TX, November 5, 2016. ©2016 Association for Computational Linguistics

gle dialog agent and requires new methods to develop decision-making algorithms to judiciously switch amongst various systems while creating a homogenous users experience.

- *Dialog System Evaluation with Real Users*: Evaluation has always be challenging for dialog systems because inexpensive methods, (e.g. user simulator or recruited users) are often not accurate. The best evaluation, real users, is costly. DialPort will create streams of real user data, which opens the possibility of developing a principled evaluation framework for dialog systems.

## 3 Proposed Approach

The prototype DialPort system includes the user interface, remote agents/resources and the master agent.

### 3.1 User Interface

The user interface is the public front-end[1]. The audio interface uses the web-based ASR/TTS to recognize the user's speech and generate DialPort's speech output. The visual representation is a virtual agent that has animated embodiments powered by the Unity 3D Engine[2].

### 3.2 Remote Agents and Resources

A *Remote agent* is a turn-based dialog system, which inputs the ASR text output of the latest turn and returns the next system response. Every external dialog system connecting to DialPort is treated as a *remote agent*. DialPort also deals with *remote resources*, which can be any external knowledge resource, such as a database of bus schedules. DialPort is in charge of all of the dialog processing and uses the remote resources as knowledge backends in the same way as a traditional goal-oriented SDS (Raux et al., 2005).

### 3.3 The Master Agent

The *master agent* operates on a set of *remote agents* $U$, and a set of *remote resources* $R$. In order to serve information in $R$, the *master agent* has a set of primitive actions $P$, such as $request$ or $inform$. Together $P \bigcup U$ composes the available action set $A$ for the master agent. The dialog state $S$ is made up of the entire history of system output and user input and distributions over possible slot values. Given the new inputs from the user interface, the master agent updates its dialog state and generates the next system response based on its policy, $\pi : S \rightarrow A$, that will choose the action $a$ that is the most appropriate. One key note is that for $a \in U$, it takes more than one turn to finish a session, i.e. a *remote agent* usually will span several turns with the users, while $a \in P$ is primitive action that only spans for one turn. Therefore, we formulate the problem as a sequential decision making problem for Semi-Markov Decision Process (SMDP) (Sutton et al., 1999), so $a \in U$ is equivalent to a macro action. Therefore, when DialPort hands over control to a *remote agent*, the user input is directly forwarded to the remote system until the session is finished by the remote side. Core research on DialPort is about how to construct an efficient representation for $S$, and how to learn a good policy $\pi$.

### 3.4 Current Status

To date, the DialPort has connected to two *remote agents*, the dialog system at Cambridge University (Gasic et al., 2015) and a chatbot, and to two *remote resources*: Yelp food API and NOAA (National Oceanic and Atmospheric Administration) Weather API.

## 4 Evaluation

Given the data collected by DialPort, assessment has several aspects. In order to create labeled data for the first two challenges mentioned in Section 2, we developed an annotation toolkit to label the correct system responses and state variables of the dialogs. The labeled data can then be used for new models for advanced dialog state tracking and multi-agent dialog policy learning. We will also solicit subjective feedback from users after a session with the system.

## 5 Travel Funding

Two authors are respectively PhD and postdoctoral students that need travel funding.

[1]https://skylar.speech.cs.cmu.edu

[2]unity3d.com/

## References

M Gasic, Dongho Kim, Pirros Tsiakoulis, and Steve Young. 2015. Distributed dialogue policies for multi-domain statistical dialogue management. In *Acoustics, Speech and Signal Processing (ICASSP), 2015 IEEE International Conference on*, pages 5371–5375. IEEE.

Antoine Raux, Brian Langner, Dan Bohus, Alan W Black, and Maxine Eskenazi. 2005. Lets go public! taking a spoken dialog system to the real world. In *in Proc. of Interspeech 2005*. Citeseer.

Iulian V Serban, Alessandro Sordoni, Yoshua Bengio, Aaron Courville, and Joelle Pineau. 2015. Building end-to-end dialogue systems using generative hierarchical neural network models. *arXiv preprint arXiv:1507.04808*.

Richard S Sutton, Doina Precup, and Satinder Singh. 1999. Between mdps and semi-mdps: A framework for temporal abstraction in reinforcement learning. *Artificial intelligence*, 112(1):181–211.

Oriol Vinyals and Quoc Le. 2015. A neural conversational model. *arXiv preprint arXiv:1506.05869*.

Tsung-Hsien Wen, David Vandyke, Nikola Mrkšić, Milica Gašić, Lina M. Rojas-Barahona, Pei-Hao Su, Stefan Ultes, and Steve Young. 2016. A network-based end-to-end trainable task-oriented dialogue system. *arXiv preprint: 1604.04562*, April.

Jason D Williams and Geoffrey Zweig. 2016. End-to-end lstm-based dialog control optimized with supervised and reinforcement learning. *arXiv preprint arXiv:1606.01269*.

Jason Williams, Antoine Raux, Deepak Ramachandran, and Alan Black. 2013. The dialog state tracking challenge. In *Proceedings of the SIGDIAL 2013 Conference*, pages 404–413.

Tiancheng Zhao and Maxine Eskenazi. 2016. Towards end-to-end learning for dialog state tracking and management using deep reinforcement learning. *arXiv preprint arXiv:1606.02560*.

# $C^2D^2E^2$: Using Call Centers to Motivate the Use of Dialog and Diarization in Entity Extraction

**Kenneth Church, Weizhong Zhu** and **Jason Pelecanos**
IBM, Yorktown Heights, NY, USA
{kwchurch, zhuwe, jwpeleca}@us.ibm.com

## Abstract

This paper introduces a deceptively simple entity extraction task intended to encourage more interdisciplinary collaboration between fields that don't normally work together: diarization, dialog and entity extraction. Given a corpus of 1.4M call center calls, extract mentions of trouble ticket numbers. The task is challenging because first mentions need to be distinguished from confirmations to avoid undesirable repetitions. It is common for agents to say part of the ticket number, and customers confirm with a repetition. There are opportunities for dialog (given/new) and diarization (who said what) to help remove repetitions. New information is spoken slowly by one side of a conversation; confirmations are spoken more quickly by the other side of the conversation.

## 1 Extracting Ticket Numbers

Much has been written on extracting entities from text (Etzioni et al., 2005), and even speech (Kubala et al., 1998), but less has been written in the context of dialog (Clark and Haviland, 1977) and diarization (Tranter and Reynolds, 2006; Anguera et al., 2012; Shum, 2011). This paper describes a ticket extraction task illustrated in Table 1. The challenge is to extract a 7 byte ticket number, "902MDYK," from the dialog. Confirmations ought to improve communication, but steps need to be taken to avoid undesirable repetition in extracted entities. Dialog theory suggests it should be possible to distinguish first mentions (**bold**) from confirmations (*italics*) based on prosodic cues such as pitch, energy and duration.

| t0 | t1 | S1 | S2 |
|---|---|---|---|
| 278.16 | 281.07 | I do have the new hardware case number for you when you're ready | |
| 282.60 | 282.85 | | *okay* |
| 284.19 | 284.80 | **nine** | |
| 285.03 | 285.86 | **zero** | |
| 286.22 | 286.74 | **two** | |
| 290.82 | 291.30 | | *nine* |
| 292.87 | 293.95 | *zero two* | |
| 297.87 | 298.24 | | *okay* |
| 299.30 | 300.49 | **M. as in Mike** | |
| 301.97 | 303.56 | **D. as in delta** | |
| 304.89 | 306.31 | **Y. as in Yankee** | |
| 307.50 | 308.81 | **K. as in kilo** | |
| 310.14 | 310.57 | | *okay* |
| 310.77 | 311.70 | | *nine zero two* |
| 311.73 | 312.49 | | *M. D.* |
| 312.53 | 313.18 | | *Y. T.* |
| 313.75 | 314.21 | *correct* | |
| 314.21 | 317.28 | and thank you for calling IBM is there anything else I can assist you with | |

**Table 1:** A ticket dialog: 7 bytes (902MDYK) at 1.4 bps. First mentions (**bold**) are slower than confirmations (*italics*).

| phone matches | calls | ticket matches (edit dist) |
|---|---|---|
| 66% | 238 | 0 |
| 59% | 82 | 1 |
| 55% | 40 | 2 |
| 4.1% | 4033 | 3+ |

**Table 2:** Phone numbers are used to confirm ticket matches. Good ticket matches (top row) are confirmed more often than poor matches (bottom row). Poor matches are more common because ticket numbers are relatively rare, and most calls don't mention them.



*Proceedings of EMNLP 2016 Workshop on Uphill Battles in Language Processing: Scaling Early Achievements to Robust Methods*, pages 35–38,
Austin, TX, November 5, 2016. 

In Table 1, "zero two" was 55% slower the first time than the second (1.7 vs. 1.1 seconds).

Much of Table 1 was produced by machine, using tools that are currently available for public use, or will be available soon. Words came from ASR (automatic speech recognition) and speaker labels (S1 and S2) from diarization.[1] We plan to label **bold** and *italics* automatically, but for now, that was done by hand.

It is remarkable how hard it is to transmit ticket numbers. In this case, it takes 39 seconds to transmit 7 bytes, "902MDYK," a mere 1.4 bps (bits per second).[2] Agents are well aware of the difficulty of the task. In Table 1, the agent says the first three digits slowly in citation form (more like isolated digits than continuous speech) (Moon, 1991). Citation form should be helpful, though in practice, ASR is trained on continuous speech, and consequently struggles with citation form.

After a few back-and-forth confirmations, the customer confirms the first three digits with a backchannel (Ward and Tsukahara, 2000) "okay," enabling the agent to continue transmitting the last four bytes, "MDYK," slowly at a byte/sec or less, using a combination of military and conventional spelling: in Mike," "D. as in delta," etc. When we discuss Figure 1, we will refer to this strategy as *slow mode*. If the agent was speaking to another agent, she would say, "Mike delta Yankee kilo," quickly with no intervening silences. We will refer to this strategy as *fast mode*.

Finally, the customer ends the exchange with another backchannel "okay," followed by a quick repetition of all 7 bytes. Again we see that first mentions (**bold**) take more time than subsequent mentions (*italics*). In Table 1, the **bold** first mention of "902MDYK" takes $12.1 = 286.74 - 284.19 + 308.81 - 299.30$ seconds, which is considerably longer than the customer's confirmation in *italics*: $2.4 = 313.18 - 310.77$ seconds.

Ticket numbers are also hard for machines. ASR errors don't help. For example, the final "K" in the final repetition was misheard by the machine as "T."

[1]The ASR tools are currently available for public use at: https://www.ibm.com/watson/developercloud/text-to-speech.html, and diarization will be released soon.

[2]The estimate of 1.4 bps would be even worse if we included opportunities for compressing tickets to less than 7 bytes.

| t0 | transcript |
|---|---|
| 344.01 | and I do have a hardware case number whenever you're ready for it |
| 348.86 | hang on just one moment |
| 353.65 | okay go ahead that will be Alfa zero nine |
| 358.18 | the number two |
| 359.85 | golf Victor Juliet |
| 363.55 | I'm sorry what was after golf |
| 366.46 | golf and then V. as in Victor J. as in Juliet |
| 370.28 | okay |
| 371.86 | Alfa zero niner two golf Victor Juliet that is correct Sir you can't do anything else for today |

**Table 3:** An example with a retransmission: 1.7 bits per second to transmit "A082GVJ"

After listening to the audio, it isn't clear if a human could get this right without context because the customer is speaking quickly with an accent. Nevertheless, the confirmation, "correct," makes it clear that the agent believes the dialog was successfully concluded and there is no need for additional confirmations/corrections. Although it is tempting to work on ASR errors forever, we believe there are bigger opportunities for dialog and diarization.

## 2 Communication Speed

The corpus can be used to measure factors that impact communication speed: given/new, familiarity, shared conventions, dialects, experience, corrections, etc. In Table 1, first mentions are slower than subsequent mentions. Disfluencies (Hindle, 1983) and corrections ("I'm sorry what was after golf") take even more time, as illustrated in Table 3.

Figure 1 shows that familiar phone numbers are quicker than less familiar ticket numbers, especially in slow mode, where each letter is expressed as a separate intonation phrase. Agents speed up when talking to other agents, and slow down for customers, especially when customers need more time. Agents have more experience than customers and are therefore faster.

Agents tend to use slow mode when speaking with customers, especially the first time they say the ticket number. Table 1 showed an example of slow mode. Fast mode tends to be used for confirmations, or when agents are speaking with other agents. Figure 1 shows that fast mode is faster than slow mode, as one would expect.

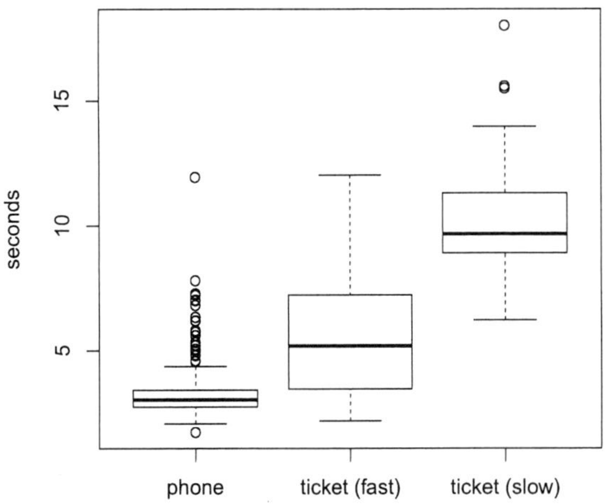


**Figure 1:** Time to say phone numbers and tickets, computed over a sample of 552 simple/robust matches. The plot shows that phone numbers are faster than ticket numbers. Ticket numbers are typically spoken in one of two ways which we call *fast mode* and *slow mode*. The plot shows that fast mode is faster than slow mode, as one would expect.

Figure 1 gives an optimistic lower bound view of times. The figure was computed over a small sample of 552 calls where simple (robust) matching methods were sufficient to find the endpoints of the match in the audio. Tables 1 and 3 demonstrate that total times tend to be much longer because of factors not included in Figure 1 such as prompts, confirmations and retransmissions.

Shared knowledge helps. Phone numbers are quicker than tickets because everyone knows their own phone number. In addition, everyone knows that phone numbers are typically 10 digits, parsed: $3+3+4$. Communication slows down when phone numbers are expressed in unfamiliar ways such as "double nine" and "triple zero," common in Indian English and Australian English, but not American English.

## 3 Materials

We are working with a call center corpus of 1.4M calls. Table 4 shows call duration by number of speakers. The average call is 5.6 minutes, but most calls are shorter than average, and a few calls are much longer than average. The 50th, 95th and 99th percentiles are 4, 15 and 31 minutes, respectively. The longer calls are likely to involve one or more transfers, and therefore, longer calls tend to have more speakers.

| Speakers | Calls | Seconds/Call |
|---|---|---|
| 0 | 565 | 20 |
| 1 | 405 | 61 |
| 2 | 5021 | 342 |
| 3 | 837 | 533 |
| 4 | 107 | 986 |
| 5 | 22 | 1121 |
| 6+ | 13 | 1166 |

**Table 4:** Most of our calls have two speakers, a customer and an agent, though some have more speakers and some have less. The duration of the call tends to increase with the number of speakers. These counts were computed from a relatively small sample of nearly 7k calls that were manually transcribed.

A relatively small sample of almost 7k calls was transcribed by a human transcription service, mainly to measure WER (word error rates) for recognition, but can also measure diarization errors. Unfortunately, ground truth is hard to come by for entity extraction because we didn't ask the service to extract phone numbers and tickets.

Heuristics are introduced to overcome this deficiency. The first 4-5 bytes of the ticket are predictable from side information (timestamps), not available to the dialog participants. Edit distance is used to match the rest with tickets in a database. Matches are confirmed by comparing phone numbers in the database with phone numbers extracted from the audio. Table 2 shows good ticket matches (top row) are confirmed more often than poor matches (bottom row).[3] Given these confirmed matches, future work will label **bold** and *italics* automatically. An annotated corpus of this kind will motivate future work on the use of dialog and diarization in entity extraction.

[3]The phone matching heuristic is imperfect in a couple of ways. The top row is far from 100% because the customer may use a different phone number than what is in the database. The bottom row contains most of the calls because the entities of interest are quite rare and do not appear in most calls.

## 4 Conclusions

This paper introduced a deceptively simple entity extraction task intended to encourage more interdisciplinary collaboration between fields that don't normally work together: diarization, dialog and entity extraction. First mentions need to be distinguished from confirmations to avoid undesirable repetition in extracted entities. Dialog theory suggests the use of prosodic cues to distinguish marked first mentions from unmarked subsequent mentions. We saw in Table 1 that first mentions (**bold**) tend to be slower than subsequent confirmations (*italics*).

It also helps to determine who said what (diarization), because new information tends to come from one side of a conversation, and confirmations from the other side. While our corpus of 1.4M calls cannot be shared for obvious privacy concerns, the ASR and diarization tools are currently available for public use (or will be available soon). While much has been written on given/new, this corpus-based approach should help establish more precise numerical conclusions in future work.

The corpus can be used to measure a number of additional factors beyond given/new that impact communication speed: familiarity, shared conventions, dialects, experience, corrections, etc. Table 3 shows an example of corrections taking even more time ("I'm sorry what was after golf"). Figure 1 shows that familiar phone numbers are quicker than less familiar ticket numbers, especially in slow mode, where each letter is expressed as a separate intonation phrase. Agents speed up when talking to other agents, and slow down for customers, especially when customers need more time. Agents have more experience than customers and are therefore faster.

## References


Xavier Anguera, Simon Bozonnet, Nicholas Evans, Corinne Fredouille, Gerald Friedland, and Oriol Vinyals. 2012. Speaker diarization: A review of recent research. *IEEE Transactions on Audio, Speech, and Language Processing*, 20(2):356–370.

Herbert H Clark and Susan E Haviland. 1977. Comprehension and the given-new contract. *Discourse production and comprehension. Discourse processes: Advances in research and theory*, 1:1–40.

Oren Etzioni, Michael Cafarella, Doug Downey, Ana-Maria Popescu, Tal Shaked, Stephen Soderland, Daniel S Weld, and Alexander Yates. 2005. Unsupervised named-entity extraction from the web: An experimental study. *Artificial intelligence*, 165(1):91–134.

Donald Hindle. 1983. Deterministic parsing of syntactic non-fluencies. In *Proceedings of the 21st annual meeting on Association for Computational Linguistics*, pages 123–128. Association for Computational Linguistics.

Francis Kubala, Richard Schwartz, Rebecca Stone, and Ralph Weischedel. 1998. Named entity extraction from speech. In *Proceedings of DARPA Broadcast News Transcription and Understanding Workshop*, pages 287–292. Citeseer.

Seung-Jae Moon. 1991. An acoustic and perceptual study of undershoot in clear and citation-form speech. *Phonetic Experimental Research at the Institute of Linguistics University of Stockholm XIV, University of Stockholm, Institute of Linguistics*, pages 153–156.

Stephen Shum. 2011. *Unsupervised methods for speaker diarization*. Ph.D. thesis, Massachusetts Institute of Technology.

Sue E Tranter and Douglas A Reynolds. 2006. An overview of automatic speaker diarization systems. *IEEE Transactions on Audio, Speech, and Language Processing*, 14(5):1557–1565.

Nigel Ward and Wataru Tsukahara. 2000. Prosodic features which cue back-channel responses in english and japanese. *Journal of pragmatics*, 32(8):1177–1207.

# Visualizing the Content of a Children's Story in a Virtual World: Lessons Learned

**Quynh Ngoc Thi Do**[1], **Steven Bethard**[2], **Marie-Francine Moens**[1]
[1]Katholieke Universiteit Leuven, Belgium
[2]University of Arizona, United States
quynhngocthi.do@cs.kuleuven.be
bethard@email.arizona.edu
sien.moens@cs.kuleuven.be

## Abstract

We present the problem of "bringing text to life" via 3D interactive storytelling, where natural language processing (NLP) techniques are used to transform narrative text into events in a virtual world that the user can interact with. This is a challenging problem, which requires deep understanding of the semantics of a story and the ability to ground those semantic elements to the actors and events of the 3D world's graphical engine. We show how this problem has motivated interesting extensions to some classic NLP tasks, identify some of the key lessons learned from the work so far, and propose some future research directions.

## 1 Introduction

Our primary goal is to take as input natural language text, such as children's stories, translate the text into formal knowledge that represents the actions, actors, plots, and surrounding world, and render this formal representation as virtual 3D worlds via a graphical engine. We believe that translating text to another modality (in our case, a visual modality) is a good test case for evaluating language understanding systems.

We have developed an initial approach to this text-to-virtual-world translation problem based on a probabilistic graphical model that maps text and its semantic annotations (generated by more traditional NLP modules, like semantic role labelers or coreference resolvers) to the knowledge representation of the graphical engine, which is defined in predicate logic. In the process, we discovered several failings of traditional NLP systems when faced with this task:

**Semantic Role Labeling** We observed that current state-of-the-art semantic role labeling (SRL) systems perform poorly on children's stories, failing to recognize many of the expressed argument roles. Much of this is due to the domain mismatch between the available training data (primarily newswire) and our evaluation (stories for 3D visualization).

To address this, we introduced a technique based on recurrent neural networks for automatically generating additional training data that was similar to the target domain (Do et al., 2014; Do et al., 2015b). For each selected word (predicate, argument head word) from the source domain, a list of replacement words from the target domain which we believe can occur at the same position as the selected word, are generated by using a recurrent neural network (RNN) language model (Mikolov et al., 2010). In addition, linguistic resources such as part of speech tags, WordNet (Miller, 1995), and VerbNet (Schuler, 2005), are used as filters to select the best replacement words.

We primarily targeted improving the results of the four circumstance roles AM-LOC, AM-TMP, AM-MNR and AM-DIR, which are important for semantic frame understanding but not well recognized by standard SRL systems. New training examples were generated specifically for the four selected roles. In an experiment with the out-of-domain setting of the CoNLL 2009 shared task and the SRL system of (Björkelund et al., 2009), training the semantic role labeller on the expanded training data outperforms the



*Proceedings of EMNLP 2016 Workshop on Uphill Battles in Language Processing: Scaling Early Achievements to Robust Methods*, pages 39–42,
Austin, TX, November 5, 2016. ©2016 Association for Computational Linguistics

model trained on the original training data by +3.36%, +2.77%, +2.84% and +14% F1 over the roles AM-LOC, AM-TMP, AM-MNR and AM-DIR respectively (Do et al., 2015b), but we still need linguistic resources to filter the words obtained by the language model. In an experiment where the same model was again trained on CoNLL 2009 training data, but the RNN training included a collection of 252 children stories (mostly fairy tales), we obtained F1 gains of +9.19,% +7.67%, +17.92% and +7.84% respectively over the four selected roles AM-LOC, AM-TMP, AM-MNR and AM-DIR, when testing on the story "The Day Tuk Became a Hunter" (Ronald and Carol, 1967) (Do et al., 2014).

**Coreference Resolution** We observed that current state-of-the-art coreference resolution systems are ignorant of some constraints that are important in storytelling. For example, a character is often first presented as an indefinite noun phrase (such as "a woman"), then later as a definite noun phrase (such as "the woman"), but this change in definiteness often resulted on missed coreference links.

To address this, we replaced the inference of the Berkeley coreference resolution system (Durrett and Klein, 2013) with a global inference algorithm which incorporated narrative specific constraints through integer linear programming (Do et al., 2015a). Our formulation models three phenomena that are important for short narrative stories: local discourse coherence, which we model via centering theory constraints, speaker-listener relations, which we model via direct speech act constraints, and character-naming, which we model via definite noun phrase and exact match constraints. When testing on the UMIREC[1] and N2[2] corpora with the coreference resolution system of (Durrett and Klein, 2013) trained on OntoNotes[3], our inference substantially improves the original inference on the CoNLL 2011 AVG score by +5.42 (for UMIREC) and +5.22 (for N2) points when using gold mentions and by +1.15 (for UMIREC) and +2.36 (for N2) points when using predicted mentions. When testing on the story "The Day Tuk Became a Hunter" (Ronald and Carol, 1967), our inference outperforms the original inference by 4.46 points on the CoNLL 2011 AVG score[4].

Having corrected some of the more serious failures of NLP systems on stories, we turn to the problem of mapping the semantic analysis of these NLP systems to the knowledge representation of the graphical engine. Our initial approach is implemented as a probabilistic graphical model, where the input is a sentence and its (probabilistic) semantic and coreference annotations, and the output is a set of logical predicate-argument structures. Each structure represents an action and the parameters of that action (e.g., person/object performing the action, location of the action). The domain is bounded by a finite set of actions, actors and objects, representable by the graphical environment. In our implementation, decoding of the model is done through an efficient formulation of a genetic algorithm that exploits conditional independence (Alazzam and Lewis III, 2013) and improves parallel scalability.

In an evaluation on three stories ("The Day Tuk Became a Hunter" (Ronald and Carol, 1967), "The Bear and the Travellers"[5], and "The First Tears"[6]), this model achieved F1 scores of 81% on recognizing the correct graphical engine actions, and above 60% on recognizing the correct action parameters (Ludwig et al., Under review). Example scenes generated by the MUSE software are shown in Figure 1, and a web-based demonstration can be accessed at `http://roshi.cs.kuleuven.be/muse_demon/`.

## 2 Lessons learned

Studying the problem of translating natural language narratives to 3D interactive stories has been instructive about the capabilities of current natural processing for language understanding and the battles that still have to be fought. The truthful rendering of language content in a virtual world acts as a testbed for

[1] `http://dspace.mit.edu/handle/1721.1/57507`

[2] `http://dspace.mit.edu/handle/1721.1/85893`

[3] `https://catalog.ldc.upenn.edu/LDC2011T03`

[4] We only evaluate the entities that are available in our virtual domain such as tuk, father, mother, bear, sister, igloo, sled, etc.

[5] `http://fairytalesoftheworld.com/quick-reads/the-bear-and-the-travellers/`

[6] `http://americanfolklore.net/folklore/2010/09/the\_first\_tears.html`

**Figure 1:** MUSE-generated scenes from "The Day Tuk Became a Hunter" (Ludwig et al., Under review).

natural language understanding, making this multimodal translation a real-life evaluation task.

On the positive side, some NLP tasks such as semantic role labeling and coreference resolution proved to be useful for instantiating the correct action frames in the virtual world with their correct actors. However, some NLP tasks that we imagined would be important turned out not to be. For example, temporal relation recognition was not very important, since children's stories have simpler timelines, and since the constraints of the actions in the 3D interactive storytelling representation could sometimes exclude the inappropriate interpretations. Moreover, across all of the NLP tasks, we saw significant drops in performance when applied to narratives like children's stories. While we introduced solutions to some of these problems, much work remains to be done to achieve easy and effective transfer of the learning models to other target texts.

Given the almost complete lack of training data for translating children's stories to the representations needed by the graphical engine (we only used two quite unrelated annotated stories to optimize the inference in the Bayesian network when our system parsed a test story), we had to rely on a pipelined approach. In this way we could exploit the knowledge obtained by the semantic role labeler and coreference resolver, which were trained on other annotated texts and adapted by the novel methods described above. The Bayesian framework of the probabilistic graphical model allows it to realize the most plausible mapping or translation to a knowledge representation given the provided evidences obtained from the features in a sentence and a previous sentence, the (probabilistic) outcome of the semantic role labeler and the (probabilistic) outcome of the coreference resolver, and to model dependencies between the variables of the network. This Bayesian framework for evidence combination makes it possible to recover from errors made by the semantic role labeler or coreference resolver.

Our most striking finding was that the text leaves a large part of its content implicit, but this content is actually needed for a truthful rendering of the text in the virtual world. For instance, often the action words used in the story were more abstract than the actions defined by the graphical engine (e.g., "take care" in reference to a knife, where actually "sharpen" was meant). Sometimes using word similarities based on embeddings (Mikolov et al., 2013) helped in such cases, but more often the meaning of such abstract words depends on the specific previous discourse, which is not captured by general embeddings. Adapting the embeddings, which are trained on a large corpus to the specific discourse context as is done in (Deschacht et al., 2012) is advisable. Moreover, certain content was not mentioned in the text, but a human could infer. For example, given "Tuk and his father tied the last things on the sled and then set off," a human would infer that the two people most likely sat down on the sled. Such knowledge is important for rendering a believable 3D interactive story, but can hardly be inferred from text data, instead needing grounding in the real world, perhaps captured by other modalities, such as images.

Another problem we encountered was scalability.

If the goal is to allow users to bring any text "to life", then all of the parsing and translation to the 3D world needs to happen online. Although the computational complexity when the machine comprehends the story is reduced by limiting the possible actions and actors (e.g., characters, objects) to the ones mentioned in the story and the ones inferred, parsing of the story is still slow. But even with the genetic algorithm inspired parallel processing we introduced, our graphical model is still too slow to operate in an online environment. Instead of considering parallel processing, it would be interesting to give priority to the most likely interpretation based on event language models (Do et al., Under review).

Finally, while working closely with researchers in 3D interactive storytelling, we learned that there is little consistency across designers of graphical worlds on the structure of basic actions, actors, objects, etc. Thus a model that has been trained to translate stories that take place in one digital world will produce invalid representations for other digital worlds. Generalizing across different digital worlds is a challenging but interesting future direction. Proposing standards could make a major impact in this field, and in addition could promote cross-modal translation between language and graphical content. We witness an increasing interest in easy to program languages for robotics that operate in virtual worlds (e.g., Mindstorms, ROBOTC) and in formalizing knowledge of virtual words by ontologies (Mezati et al., 2015). Although valuable, such approaches translate yet to another human made language. If we really want to test language understanding in a real-life setting, translation to perceptual images and video might be more suited, but more difficult to realize unless we find a way of composing realistic images and video out of primitive visual patterns.

## Acknowledgments

This work was funded by the EU ICT FP7 FET project "Machine Understanding for interactive StorytElling" (MUSE). We thank the anonymous reviewers for their valuable comments.

## References

Azmi Alazzam and Harold W. Lewis III. 2013. A new optimization algorithm for combinatorial problems. *International Journal of Advanced Research in Artificial Intelligence, IJARAI*, 2(5).

Anders Björkelund, Love Hafdell, and Pierre Nugues. 2009. Multilingual semantic role labeling. In *Proceedings of the Thirteenth Conference on Computational Natural Language Learning: Shared Task*, CoNLL '09, pages 43–48, Stroudsburg, PA, USA. ACL.

Koen Deschacht, Jan De Belder, and Marie-Francine Moens. 2012. The latent words language model. *Computer Speech and Language*, 26(5):384–409, October.

Quynh Ngoc Thi Do, Steven Bethard, and Marie-Francine Moens. 2014. Text mining for open domain semi-supervised semantic role labeling. In *DMNLP@ PKDD/ECML*, pages 33–48.

Quynh Ngoc Thi Do, Steven Bethard, and Marie-Francine Moens. 2015a. Adapting coreference resolution for narrative processing. In *Proceedings of EMNLP 2015*.

Quynh Ngoc Thi Do, Steven Bethard, and Marie-Francine Moens. 2015b. Domain adaptation in semantic role labeling using a neural language model and linguistic resources. *IEEE/ACM Transactions on Audio, Speech & Language Processing*, 23(11):1812–1823.

Quynh Ngoc Thi Do, Steven Bethard, and Marie-Francine Moens. Recurrent neural semantic frame language model. Under review.

Greg Durrett and Dan Klein. 2013. Easy victories and uphill battles in coreference resolution. In *Proceedings of EMNLP 2013*.

Oswaldo Ludwig, Do Quynh Thi Ngoc, Smith Cameron, Cavazza Marc, and Moens Marie-Francine. Translating written stories into virtual reality. Under review.

Messaoud Mezati, Foudil Cherif, Cdric Sanza, and Vronique Gaildrat. 2015. An ontology for semantic modelling of virtual world. *International Journal of Artificial Intelligence & Applications*, 6(1):65–74, janvier.

Tomas Mikolov, Martin Karafit, Lukas Burget, Jan Cernock, and Sanjeev Khudanpur. 2010. Recurrent neural network based language model. In Takao Kobayashi, Keikichi Hirose, and Satoshi Nakamura, editors, *INTERSPEECH*, pages 1045–1048. ISCA.

Tomas Mikolov, Kai Chen, Greg Corrado, and Jeffrey Dean. 2013. Efficient estimation of word representations in vector space. *arXiv preprint arXiv:1301.3781*.

George A. Miller. 1995. Wordnet: A lexical database for English. *Commun. ACM*, 38(11):39–41, November.

Melzack Ronald and Jones Carol. 1967. *The Day Tuk Became a Hunter and Other Eskimo Stories*. Dodd, Mead New York.

Karin Kipper Schuler. 2005. *Verbnet: A broad-coverage, comprehensive verb lexicon*. Ph.D. thesis, Philadelphia, PA, USA. AAI3179808.

# Stylistic Transfer in Natural Language Generation Systems Using Recurrent Neural Networks

**Jad Kabbara** and **Jackie Chi Kit Cheung**
School of Computer Science
McGill University
Montreal, QC, Canada
jad@cs.mcgill.ca jcheung@cs.mcgill.ca

## Abstract

Linguistic style conveys the social context in which communication occurs and defines particular ways of using language to engage with the audiences to which the text is accessible. In this work, we are interested in the task of stylistic transfer in natural language generation (NLG) systems, which could have applications in the dissemination of knowledge across styles, automatic summarization and author obfuscation. The main challenges in this task involve the lack of parallel training data and the difficulty in using stylistic features to control generation. To address these challenges, we plan to investigate neural network approaches to NLG to automatically learn and incorporate stylistic features in the process of language generation. We identify several evaluation criteria, and propose manual and automatic evaluation approaches.

## 1 Introduction

*Linguistic style* is an integral aspect of natural language communication. It conveys the social context in which communication occurs and defines particular ways of using language to engage with the audiences to which the text is accessible.

In this work, we examine the task of stylistic transfer in NLG systems; that is, changing the style or genre of a passage while preserving its semantic content. For example, given texts written in one genre, such as Shakespearean texts, we would like a system that can convert it into another, say, that of simple English Wikipedia. Currently, most knowledge available in textual form is locked into the particular data collection in which it is found. An automatic stylistic transfer system would allow that information to be more generally disseminated. For example, technical articles could be rewritten into a form that is accessible to a broader audience. Alternatively, stylistic transfer could also be useful for security or privacy purposes, such as in author obfuscation, where the style of the text is changed in order to mask the identity of the original author.

One of the main research challenges in stylistic transfer is the difficulty in using linguistic features to signal a certain style. Previous work in computational stylistics have identified a number of stylistic cues (e.g., passive vs active sentences, repetitive usage of pronouns, ratio of adjectives to nouns, and frequency of uncommon nouns). However, it is unclear how a system would transfer this knowledge into controlling realization decisions in an NLG system. A second challenge is that it is difficult and expensive to obtain adequate training data. Given the large number of stylistic categories, it seems infeasible to collect parallel texts for all, or even a substantial number of style pairs. Thus, we cannot directly cast this as a machine translation problem in a standard supervised setting.

Recent advances in deep learning provide an opportunity to address these problems. Work in image recognition using deep learning approaches has shown that it is possible to learn representations that separate aspects of the object from the identity of the object. For example, it is possible to learn features that represent the pose of a face (Cheung et al., 2014) or the direction of a chair (Yang et al., 2015), in order to generate images of faces/chairs with new



*Proceedings of EMNLP 2016 Workshop on Uphill Battles in Language Processing: Scaling Early Achievements to Robust Methods*, pages 43–47, Austin, TX, November 5, 2016. 

poses/directions. We plan to design similar recurrent neural network architectures to disentangle the style from the semantic content in text. This setup not only requires less hand-engineering of features, but also allows us to frame stylistic transfer as a weakly supervised problem without parallel data, in which the model learns to disentangle and recombine latent representations of style and semantic content in order to generate output text in the desired style.

In the rest of the paper, we discuss our plans to investigate stylistic transfer with neural networks in more detail. We will also propose several evaluation criteria for stylistic transfer and discuss evaluation methodologies using human user studies.

## 2 Related Work

Capturing stylistic variation is a long-standing problem in NLP. Sekine (1997) and Ratnaparkhi (1999) consider the different categories in the Brown corpus to be domains. These include *general fiction, romance and love story, press: reportage.* Gildea (2001), on the other hand, refers to these categories as genres. Different NLP sub-communities use the terms *domain, style* and *genre* to denote slightly different concepts (Lee, 2001). From a linguistic point of view, domains could be thought of as broad *subject fields*, while genre can be seen as a category assigned on the basis of external criteria such as intended audience, purpose, and activity type. Style conveys the social context in which communication occurs and define particular ways of using language to engage with the audiences to which the text is accessible. Some linguists would argue that style and domain are two attributes characterizing genre (e.g., (Lee, 2001)) while others view genre and domain as aspects representing style (e.g., (Moessner, 2001)).

The notion of genre has been the focus of related NLP tasks. In genre classification (Petrenz and Webber, 2011; Sharoff et al., 2010; Feldman et al., 2009), the task is to categorize the text into one of several genres. In author identification (Houvardas and Stamatatos, 2006; Chaski, 2001), the goal is to identify the author of a text, while author obfuscation (Kacmarcik and Gamon, 2006; Juola and Vescovi, 2011) consists in modifying aspects of the texts so that forensic analysis fails to reveal the identity of the author.

In (Pavlick and Tetreault, 2016), an analysis of formality in online written communication is presented. A set of linguistic features is proposed based on a study of human perceptions of formality across multiple genres. Those features are fed to a statistical model that classifies texts as having a formal or informal style. At the lexical level, Brooke et al. (2010) focused on constructing lexicons of formality that can be used in tasks such as genre classification or sentiment analysis. In (Inkpen and Hirst, 2004), a set list of near-synonyms is given for a target word, and one synonym is selected based on several types of preferences, e.g., stylistic (degree of formality). We aim to generalize this work beyond the lexical level.

A similar work is that of Xu et al. (2012) which propose using phrase-based machine translation systems to carry out paraphrasing while targeting a particular writing style. Since the problem is framed as a machine translation problem, it relies on parallel data where the source "language" is the original text to be paraphrased–in that case, Shakespeare texts–and the "translation" is the equivalent modern English version of those Shakespeare texts. Accordingly, for each source sentence, there exists a parallel sentence having the target style. They also present some baselines which do not make use of parallel sentences and instead rely on manually compiled dictionaries of expressions commonly found in Shakespearean English. In a more recent work, Sennrich et al. (2016) carry out translation from English to German while controlling the degree of politeness. This is done in the context of neural machine translation by adding side constraints. Specifically, they mark up the source language of the training data (in this case, English) with a feature that encodes the use of honorifics seen in the target language (in this case, German). This allows them to control the honorifics that are produced at test time.

## 3 Proposed Approach

Recently, RNN-based models have been successfully used in machine translation (Cho et al., 2014b; Cho et al., 2014a; Sutskever et al., 2014) and dialogue systems (Wen et al., 2015). Thus, we propose to use an LSTM-based RNN model based on the encoder-decoder structure (Cho et al., 2014b) to automatically process stylistic nuances instead of hand-engineering features. The model is a variant of an autoencoder where the latent representation has two separate components: one for style and one for content. The learned *stylistic* features would be distinct from the *content* features and specific to each style category, such that they can be swapped between training and testing models to perform stylistic transfer. The separation, or *disentanglement*, between stylistic and content features is reinforced by modifying the training objective from (Cho et al., 2014b) that maximizes the conditional log-likelihood (of the output given the input). Instead, our model is trained to maximize a training objective that also includes a cross-covariance term dedicated for the disentanglement.

At a high level, our proposed approach consists of the following steps:

1. For a given style transfer task between two styles A and B, we will first collect relevant corpora for each of those styles.

2. Next, we will train the model on each of the styles (separately). This would allow the system to *disentangle* the content features from the stylistic features. At the end of this step, we will have (separately) the features that characterize styles A and those that characterize style B.

3. During the testing phase, for a transfer, say, from style A to style B, the system is fed texts having style A while the stylistic latent variables of the model are fixed to be those learned for style B (from the previous step). This would force the model to generate text using style B. For a transfer from style B to A, the system is fed texts having style B and we fix the stylistic latent variables of the model to be those learned for style A.

We intend to apply the model to datasets with reasonably differing styles between training and testing. Examples include the complete works of Shakespeare[1], the Wikpedia Kaggle dataset [2], the Oxford Text Archive (literary texts) [3], and Twitter data. A future research direction would be to further improve the system to process texts that have differing but similar styles.

[1]http://norvig.com/ngrams/shakespeare.txt

[2]https://www.kaggle.com/c/wikichallenge/Data

## 4 Evaluation

We first present a simple example that shows the input and output of the system during the testing phase. Assuming the system was trained on texts taken from Simple English Wikipedia, it would learn the stylistic features that are particular to that genre. During the testing phase, if we feed the system the following sentence taken from Shakespeare's play As You Like It (Act 1, Scene 1):

> *As I remember, Adam, it was upon this fashion bequeathed me by will but poor a thousand crowns, and, as thou sayest, charged my brother on his blessing to breed me well. And there begins my sadness.*

we expect the system to produce a version that might be similar to the following:

> *I remember, Adam, that's exactly why my father only left me a thousand crowns in his will. And as you know, my father asked my brother to make sure that I was brought up well. And that's where my sadness begins.*

We see three main criteria for the evaluation of stylistic transfer systems: **soundness** (i.e., the generated texts being textually entailed with the original version), **coherence** (e.g., free of grammatical errors, proper word usage, etc.), and **effectiveness** (i.e., the generated texts actually match the desired style). We propose to evaluate systems using both human and automatic evaluations. Snippets of original and generated texts will be sampled and reviewed by human evaluators, who will judge them on these three criteria using Likert ratings. This type of evaluation technique is also used in related tasks such as to evaluate author obfuscation systems (Stamatatos et al., 2015). A future research direction is

[3]https://ota.ox.ac.uk/

to investigate automatic evaluation measures similar to ROUGE and BLEU, which compare the content of the generated text against human-written gold standards using word or n-gram overlap.

## 5 Conclusion

We present stylistic transfer as a challenging generation task. Our proposed research will address challenges to the task, such as the lack of parallel training data and the difficulty of defining features that represent style. We will exploit deep learning models to extract stylistic features that are relevant to generation without requiring explicit parallel training data between the source and the target styles. We plan to evaluate our methods using human judgments, according to criteria that we propose, derived from related tasks.

## References


Julian Brooke, Tong Wang, and Graeme Hirst. 2010. Automatic acquisition of lexical formality. In *Proceedings of the 23rd International Conference on Computational Linguistics: Posters*, pages 90–98. Association for Computational Linguistics.

Carole E Chaski. 2001. Empirical evaluations of language-based author identification techniques. *Forensic Linguistics*, 8:1–65.

Brian Cheung, Jesse A Livezey, Arjun K Bansal, and Bruno A Olshausen. 2014. Discovering hidden factors of variation in deep networks. *arXiv preprint arXiv:1412.6583*.

Kyunghyun Cho, Bart van Merriënboer, Dzmitry Bahdanau, and Yoshua Bengio. 2014a. On the properties of neural machine translation: Encoder-decoder approaches. *arXiv preprint arXiv:1409.1259*.

Kyunghyun Cho, Bart van Merrienboer, Caglar Gulcehre, Dzmitry Bahdanau, Fethi Bougares, Holger Schwenk, and Yoshua Bengio. 2014b. Learning phrase representations using rnn encoder–decoder for statistical machine translation. In *Proceedings of the 2014 Conference on Empirical Methods in Natural Language Processing (EMNLP)*, pages 1724–1734, Doha, Qatar, October. Association for Computational Linguistics.

Sergey Feldman, Marius A Marin, Mari Ostendorf, and Maya R Gupta. 2009. Part-of-speech histograms for genre classification of text. In *2009 IEEE International Conference on Acoustics, Speech and Signal Processing*, pages 4781–4784. IEEE.

Daniel Gildea. 2001. Corpus variation and parser performance. In *Proceedings of the 2001 Conference on Empirical Methods in Natural Language Processing*, pages 167–202.

John Houvardas and Efstathios Stamatatos. 2006. N-gram feature selection for authorship identification. In *International Conference on Artificial Intelligence: Methodology, Systems, and Applications*, pages 77–86. Springer.

Diana Zaiu Inkpen and Graeme Hirst. 2004. Near-synonym choice in natural language generation. In *Recent Advances in Natural Language Processing*, volume 3, pages 141–152.

Patrick Juola and Darren Vescovi. 2011. Analyzing stylometric approaches to author obfuscation. In *IFIP International Conference on Digital Forensics*, pages 115–125. Springer.

Gary Kacmarcik and Michael Gamon. 2006. Obfuscating document stylometry to preserve author anonymity. In *Proceedings of the COLING/ACL on Main conference poster sessions*, pages 444–451. Association for Computational Linguistics.

David Y.W. Lee. 2001. Genres, registers, text types, domains and styles: Clarifying the concepts and navigating a path through the bnc jungle. *Language Learning and Technology*, 5(3):37–72, September.

Lilo Moessner. 2001. Genre, text type, style, register: A terminological maze? *European Journal of English Studies*, 5(2):131–138.

Ellie Pavlick and Joel Tetreault. 2016. An empirical analysis of formality in online communication. *Transactions of the Association for Computational Linguistics*, 4:61–74.

Philipp Petrenz and Bonnie Webber. 2011. Stable classification of text genres. *Computational Linguistics*, 37(2):385–393.

Adwait Ratnaparkhi. 1999. Learning to parse natural language with maximum entropy models. *Machine learning*, 34(1-3):151–175.

Satoshi Sekine. 1997. The domain dependence of parsing. In *Proceedings of the fifth conference on Applied natural language processing*, pages 96–102. Association for Computational Linguistics.

Rico Sennrich, Barry Haddow, and Alexandra Birch. 2016. Controlling politeness in neural machine translation via side constraints. In *Proceedings of the 2016 Conference of the North American Chapter of the Association for Computational Linguistics: Human Language Technologies*, pages 35–40, San Diego, California, June. Association for Computational Linguistics.

Serge Sharoff, Zhili Wu, and Katja Markert. 2010. The web library of babel: evaluating genre collections. In *LREC*. Citeseer.

Efstathios Stamatatos, Martin Potthast, Francisco Rangel, Paolo Rosso, and Benno Stein. 2015.

Overview of the pan/clef 2015 evaluation lab. In *International Conference of the Cross-Language Evaluation Forum for European Languages*, pages 518–538. Springer.

Ilya Sutskever, Oriol Vinyals, and Quoc VV Le. 2014. Sequence to sequence learning with neural networks. In *Advances in neural information processing systems*, pages 3104–3112.

Tsung-Hsien Wen, Milica Gasic, Nikola Mrkšić, Pei-Hao Su, David Vandyke, and Steve Young. 2015. Semantically conditioned lstm-based natural language generation for spoken dialogue systems. In *Proceedings of the 2015 Conference on Empirical Methods in Natural Language Processing*, pages 1711–1721, Lisbon, Portugal, September. Association for Computational Linguistics.

Wei Xu, Alan Ritter, William B Dolan, Ralph Grishman, and Colin Cherry. 2012. Paraphrasing for style. In *24th International Conference on Computational Linguistics, COLING 2012*.

Jimei Yang, Scott E Reed, Ming-Hsuan Yang, and Honglak Lee. 2015. Weakly-supervised disentangling with recurrent transformations for 3d view synthesis. In *Advances in Neural Information Processing Systems*, pages 1099–1107.

# Using Language Groundings for Context-Sensitive Text Prediction

**Timothy Lewis, Amy Hurst, Matthew E. Taylor, & Cynthia Matuszek**
tim22@umbc.edu | amyhurst@umbc.edu | taylorm@eecs.wsu.edu | cmat@umbc.edu

## Abstract

In this paper, we present the concept of using language groundings for context-sensitive text prediction using a semantically informed, context-aware language model. We show initial findings from a preliminary study investigating how users react to a communication interface driven by context-based prediction using a simple language model. We suggest that the results support further exploration using a more informed semantic model and more realistic context.

***Keywords***— Grounded language, context sensitive generation, predictive text

## 1 Introduction

Advances in natural language and world perception have led to a resurgence of work on the *language grounding problem.* Most work to date has focused on learning a model of language describing the world, then using it to understand novel language, e.g., following directions, (Artzi and Zettlemoyer, 2013; MacGlashan et al., 2015) or learning to understand commands in a space of plans or commands (Misra et al., 2014).

Generating language based on context is arguably more difficult, although the additional information provided by context makes this a promising area for natural language generation in general. There is a growing body of work on context-based generation in limited domains, such as sportscasting (Chen and Mooney, 2010), asking questions (Tellex et al., 2014), or generating spatial descriptions or narratives (Huo and Skubic, 2016; Rosenthal et al., 2016). In order to provide communication suggestions for users, it is not necessary to solve the problem of arbitrary natural language generation. Instead, the system must be able to provide predictions that support a predictive language interface, in which a user is continuously provided with a set of suggestions for possible speech.

We propose an approach, in which a joint linguistic/perceptual model is used to drive a predictive text tool, targeting augmentative and alternative communication (AAC) tools for wheelchair users with motor apraxia of speech. We propose to use the speaker's environment as *context* to make more relevant predictions.

Sensed context will be used to drive the probability of predictions and reduce ambiguity; for example, while "button" may refer to a fastener for clothing or a control for an electronic device, someone in front of an elevator is probably referring to the latter, which in turn focuses what they are likely to want to say. Instrumented wheelchairs can capture a large corpus of language paired with context to support development of a user-specific model trained before and during degradation of the ability to speak.

This paper discusses a pilot study using a preliminary language model with simulated context. Participants responded to scenarios using a prototype interface to communicate. Using results and observations from this user study, we hypothesize that context-based predictive lan-



*Proceedings of EMNLP 2016 Workshop on Uphill Battles in Language Processing: Scaling Early Achievements to Robust Methods*, pages 48–52,
Austin, TX, November 5, 2016. 

guage can improve usability of a predictive text interface and represents a promising direction for future work.

## 2 Approach

In grounded language acquisition, a combination of language and physical context are used to develop a language model for understanding future utterances. (Mooney, 2008) The context can be physical (depending on physical sensors, sometimes on a robot), (Fasola and Mataric, 2014) a simulation of some physical context, (Chen and Mooney, 2011) or more abstract descriptions. (Kress-Gazit and Fainekos, 2008) We propose to collect and learn from a similar set of data, with a language model targeting generation rather than understanding.

### 2.1 Corpus Collection

In order to learn a model of contextualized speech, it is necessary to collect both spoken language and context describing the environment when communication is occurring. We propose to perform this collection in three stages, from general to user-focused, as we build a better corpus and model.

*(1) Crowdsourcing* To gain a better understanding of how people may respond in different situations, Mechanical Turk will be leveraged to solicit responses from users about various scenarios. Each scenario presents a speaker with text describing a certain situation (and images when appropriate) and asked what they would say. This provides us with an initial corpus of typed responses to known scenarios. The preliminary study (see Section 3) was performed on a small-scale crowdsourced corpus.

*(2) Telepresence* For the second stage, we will use a telepresence robot (see Figure 1). The Beam robot provides insight into situations that may require assistance (for example, having the robot travel between floors of a building via the elevator, or delivering a package from one office to another). The Beam's existing video cameras and microphone/speaker interactions can be captured to provide a time-aligned corpus.

**Figure 1:** Telepresence-based context and language. *(left)* Bystanders push a button in response to a verbal request from the robot. *(right)* Video feed from the robot's sensors. In this example, the most visually salient elements of context are the elevator and people.

*(3) End Users* When a sufficiently robust model exists, we will instrument wheelchairs of proposed end users (e.g., ALS patients). This sensor array must be unobtrusive and relatively low power. This will include one or more time-of-flight Kinect 2 RGB-D cameras, an omnidirectional powered microphone, and a high-resolution camera.

### 2.2 Context Interpretation

While any feature of as environment or actions may provide important context, we will focus on gathering sensor observations describing the most salient elements of the environment. We expect this to be primarily: 1) People in the environment, who will circumscribe the set of things the user is likely to want to say; 2) Objects in the environment, including fixed objects such as elevators; and 3) The environment itself.

Identifying elements of a scene is a difficult problem; initial efforts will use crowdsourcing or other low-cost, high-speed annotation of sensor data, but the broader intention is to use recent work on automatic identification of important visual elements (Carl Vondrick, 2016) and semantic labeling. (Anand et al., 2012)

Existing efforts on building language models from observations collect and train on corpora that are targeted to a particular scenario. Because we are gathering ongoing speech in a variety of settings, we are trying to learn from non-targeted speech, where the connection between the language and the sensor observations may be tenuous or non-existent. (For example, a person may be talking about medication side effects while navigating.) Gathering data over a long period should allow irrelevant context to be weighted down in the learned model.

### 2.3 Language Learning

Our approach to text prediction inverts an existing model (Matuszek et al., 2013), in which the authors trained a joint model of language and context, and then treated language as a query against a perceived world state. In that work, the goal is to find a set of groundings in the world referred to by language $x$. The induced model is then $P(G|x, C)$, given data of the form $D = \{(x_i, C_i, G_i)|i = 1...n\}$, where each example $i$ contains a sentence $x_i$, the world context $C_i$, and the actual referent (grounding) $G_i$.

In this work, we treat perceptual context as 'input' and language as 'output.' Given a similar dataset, the model to be induced is then $P(x|G, C)$. Our intention is to learn a similar model, incorporating semantic parsing and perceptual information and giving a probability distribution over possible generated outputs, as done elsewhere (FitzGerald et al., 2013). However, our initial experiments were performed using an n-gram prediction model.

The generation goal is a list of predictions from which a user can select. Since generated predictions can range in complexity from words to full sentences, generation strategies based on certainty can be applied, where more complex constructs are generated in higher-certainty situations. In this setting, providing a top-$n$ list of results is useful, reducing the need for finding the single best generation.

## 3 Preliminary Study

For the preliminary user study, a set of four scenarios were shown to a group of fifteen participants. The scenarios asked each participant what they would say in each of four situations: a social interaction; answering questions from a doctor; asking someone to push an elevator button; and asking someone to retrieve a water bottle. The context was described to participants in text, simplifying out the question of how to represent real-world context. (See box for an example scenario and some responses.)

**You have been having stomach pains after eating each day for the past week. You are visiting your doctor, who asks how you are doing. What is your response?**

- "My stomach has been bothering me after I eat."
- "My stomach hurts whenever I eat."
- "I'm ok but I've been having stomach issues."
- "Good aside from the gut pain I'm having after eating."
- "I have been having stomach pains after eating each day for the past week."

### 3.1 Prediction Experiments

An interface was developed to test four different methods for generating predictions, of which three are novel to this work. These methods vary in the length of generated predictions: users were presented with combinations of single words, short phrases, or full sentences (see Table 1). A simulated QWERTY keyboard was available for fallback text entry. A new pool of participants were asked to use the interface to communicate responses to the same four scenarios, rather than typing responses on a keyboard.

In order to generate a predictive language model that is context driven based on these scenarios, $n$-gram models were constructed using the Presage predictive text entry program[1]. Four different prediction methods were tested using this model (see Table 1).

| Method | Corpus | W. | P. | S. |
|---|---|---|---|---|
| StdEng | Standard English | ✓ | ✓ | |
| ContWord | Contextual | ✓ | | |
| Context | Contextual | ✓ | ✓ | |
| ContSent | Contextual | ✓ | ✓ | ✓ |

**Table 1:** The four text prediction methods tested, which vary in whether they generate words (W), Phrases (P), and sentences (S), and whether they are based on an existing English corpus or a preliminary contextual corpus.

For each participant/scenario pair, the number of selections (clicks) necessary to communicate was recorded. After each participant completed the tasks, they filled out a survey about the usability of the interface, how effectively

[1] `http://presage.sourceforge.net`, 2016-08-01

they felt they were able to communicate, and the perceived speed of each entry method.

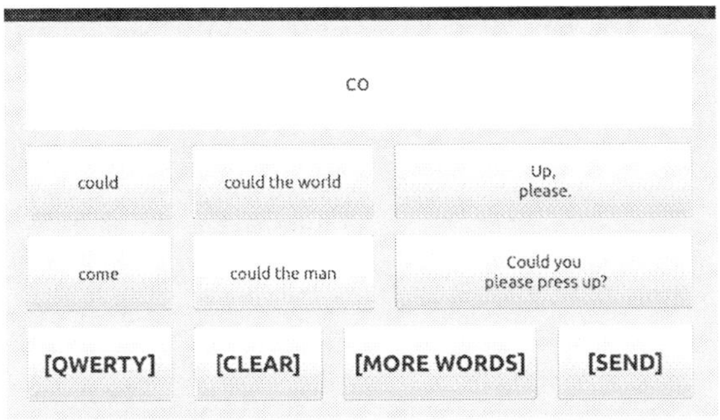


**Figure 2:** The prototype interface used in the preliminary study. The interface provides various options for text selection including full sentences and a virtual keyboard.

This pilot supported the hypothesis that users communicate faster with context-sensitive prediction (Figure 3); of the most-comparable methods, CONTEXT was faster than STDENG. While communication is fastest when complete sentences are shown, the users did not qualitatively prefer this option, underscoring the importance of personalized communication.

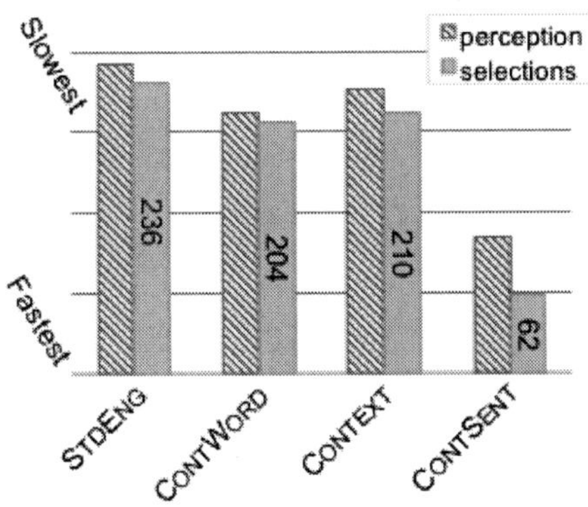


**Figure 3:** Participants' *qualitative* perception of the relative speed of different methods (green), compared to the number of selections actually used (blue). Perceived speed is shown as a weighted average of non-numeric rankings, and aligns closely with the number of selections required to complete a task.

## 4 Discussion and Future Work

We intend to pursue further experiments using more complete language and grounding models. For this, some simplifications must be addressed. The most immediate are the best way of modeling language and incorporating real-world context; this is necessary to know whether building a semantically informed, context-aware prediction model will present large gains in accuracy and acceptability. We believe this work will be able to contribute to the research community, providing leads and methods for more intelligent and usable language models. Nonetheless, while ambitious, our initial results support the belief that this approach has promise for text prediction and context-aware generation.

## References

Abhishek Anand, Hema Swetha Koppula, Thorsten Joachims, and Ashutosh Saxena. 2012. Contextually guided semantic labeling and search for three-dimensional point clouds. *The International Journal of Robotics Research*, page 0278364912461538.

Yoav Artzi and Luke Zettlemoyer. 2013. Weakly supervised learning of semantic parsers for mapping instructions to actions. *Transactions of the Association for Computational Linguistics (TACL)*, 1:49–62.

Antonio Torralba Carl Vondrick, Hamed Pirsiavash. 2016. Anticipating visual representations from unlabeled video. In *Proceedings of the IEEE Conference on Computer Vision and Pattern Recognition*.

David L Chen and Raymond J Mooney. 2010. Training a multilingual sportscaster: Using perceptual context to learn language. *Journal of Artificial Intelligence Research*, 37:397–435.

David L Chen and Raymond J Mooney. 2011. Learning to interpret natural language navigation instructions from observations. In *AAAI*, volume 2, pages 1–2.

Juan Fasola and Maja J Mataric. 2014. Interpreting instruction sequences in spatial language discourse with pragmatics towards natural human-robot interaction. In *Robotics and Automation (ICRA), 2014 IEEE International Conference on*, pages 2720–2727. IEEE.

Nicholas FitzGerald, Yoav Artzi, and Luke S Zettlemoyer. 2013. Learning distributions over logical forms for referring expression generation. In *EMNLP*, pages 1914–1925.

Zhiyu Huo and Marjorie Skubic. 2016. Natural spatial description generation for human-robot interaction in indoor environments. In *2016 IEEE*

*International Conference on Smart Computing (SMARTCOMP)*, pages 1–3. IEEE.

Hadas Kress-Gazit and Georgios E Fainekos. 2008. Translating structured English to robot controllers. *Advanced Robotics*, 22:1343–1359.

James MacGlashan, Monica Babes-Vroman, Marie desJardins, Michael Littman, Smaranda Muresan, Shawn Squire, Stefanie Tellex, Dilip Arumugam, and Lei Yang. 2015. Grounding english commands to reward functions. In *Proceedings of Robotics: Science and Systems*, Rome, Italy, July.

Cynthia Matuszek, Nicholas FitzGerald, Luke Zettlemoyer, Liefeng Bo, and Dieter Fox. 2013. A Joint Model of Language and Perception for Grounded Attribute Learning. In *Proc. of the 2012 International Conference on Machine Learning*, Edinburgh, Scotland, June.

Dipendra K Misra, Jaeyong Sung, Kevin Lee, and Ashutosh Saxena. 2014. Tell me dave: Context-sensitive grounding of natural language to mobile manipulation instructions. In *Proceedings of Robotics: Science and Systems*. Citeseer.

Raymond J Mooney. 2008. Learning to connect language and perception. In *AAAI*, pages 1598–1601.

Stephanie Rosenthal, Sai P Selvaraj, and Manuela Veloso. 2016. Verbalization: Narration of autonomous mobile robot experience. In *26th International Joint Conference on Artificial Intelligence (IJCAI16). New York City, NY.*

Stefanie Tellex, Ross Knepper, Adrian Li, Daniela Rus, and Nicholas Roy. 2014. Asking for help using inverse semantics. *Proceedings of Robotics: Science and Systems, Berkeley, USA.*

# Towards a continuous modeling of natural language domains

Sebastian Ruder[1,2], Parsa Ghaffari[2], and John G. Breslin[1]

[1]Insight Centre for Data Analytics
National University of Ireland, Galway
{sebastian.ruder,john.breslin}@insight-centre.org
[2]Aylien Ltd.
Dublin, Ireland
{sebastian,parsa}@aylien.com

## Abstract

Humans continuously adapt their style and language to a variety of domains. However, a reliable definition of 'domain' has eluded researchers thus far. Additionally, the notion of discrete domains stands in contrast to the multiplicity of heterogeneous domains that humans navigate, many of which overlap. In order to better understand the change and variation of human language, we draw on research in domain adaptation and extend the notion of discrete domains to the continuous spectrum. We propose representation learning-based models that can adapt to continuous domains and detail how these can be used to investigate variation in language. To this end, we propose to use dialogue modeling as a test bed due to its proximity to language modeling and its social component.

## 1 Introduction

The notion of domain permeates natural language and human interaction: Humans continuously vary their language depending on the context, in writing, dialogue, and speech. However, the concept of domain is ill-defined, with conflicting definitions aiming to capture the essence of what constitutes a domain. In semantics, a domain is considered a "specific area of cultural emphasis" (Oppenheimer, 2006) that entails a particular terminology, e.g. a specific sport. In sociolinguistics, a domain consists of a group of related social situations, e.g. all human activities that take place at home. In discourse a domain is a "cognitive construct (that is) created in response to a number of factors" (Douglas, 2004) and includes a variety of registers. Finally, in the context of transfer learning, a domain is defined as consisting of a feature space $\mathcal{X}$ and a marginal probability distribution $P(X)$ where $X = \{x_1, ..., x_n\}$ and $x_i$ is the $i^{th}$ feature vector (Pan and Yang, 2010).

These definitions, although pertaining to different concepts, have a commonality: They separate the world in stationary domains that have clear boundaries. However, the real world is more ambiguous. Domains permeate each other and humans navigate these changes in domain.

Consequently, it seems only natural to step away from a *discrete* notion of domain and adopt a *continuous* notion. Utterances often cannot be naturally separated into discrete domains, but often arise from a continuous underlying process that is reflected in many facets of natural language: The web contains an exponentially growing amount of data, where each document "is potentially its own domain" (McClosky et al., 2010); a second-language learner adapts their style as their command of the language improves; language changes with time and with locality; even the WSJ section of the Penn Treebank – often treated as a single domain – contains different types of documents, such as news, lists of stock prices, etc. Continuity is also an element of real-world applications: In spam detection, spammers continuously change their tactics; in sentiment analysis, sentiment is dependent on trends emerging and falling out of favor.

Drawing on research in domain adaptation, we first compare the notion of continuous natural language domains against mixtures of discrete domains and motivate the choice of using dialogue modeling



*Proceedings of EMNLP 2016 Workshop on Uphill Battles in Language Processing: Scaling Early Achievements to Robust Methods*, pages 53–57,
Austin, TX, November 5, 2016. 

as a test bed. We then present a way of representing continuous domains and show how continuous domains can be incorporated into existing models. We finally propose a framework for evaluation.

## 2 Continuous domains vs. mixtures of discrete domains

In domain adaptation, a novel target domain is traditionally assumed to be discrete and independent of the source domain (Blitzer et al., 2006). Other research uses mixtures to model the target domain based on a single (Daumé III and Marcu, 2006) or multiple discrete source domains (Mansour, 2009). We argue that modeling a novel domain as a mixture of existing domains falls short in light of three factors.

Firstly, the diversity of human language makes it unfeasible to restrict oneself to a limited number of source domains, from which all target domains are modeled. This is exemplified by the diversity of the web, which contains billions of heterogeneous websites; the Yahoo! Directory[1] famously contained thousands of hand-crafted categories in an attempt to separate these. Notably, many sub-categories were cross-linked as they could not be fully separated and websites often resided in multiple categories.

Similarly, wherever humans come together, the culmination of different profiles and interests gives rise to cliques, interest groups and niche communities that all demonstrate their own unique behaviors, unspoken rules, and memes. A mixture of existing domains fails to capture these varieties.

Secondly, using discrete domains for soft assignments relies on the assumption that the source domains are clearly defined. However, discrete labels only help to explain domains and make them interpretable, when in reality, a domain is a heterogeneous amalgam of texts. Indeed, Plank and van Noord (2011) show that selection based on human-assigned labels fares worse than using automatic domain similarity measures for parsing.

Thirdly, not only a speaker's style and command of a language are changing, but a language itself is continuously evolving. This is amplified in fast-moving media such as social platforms. Therefore, applying a discrete label to a domain merely anchors it in time. A probabilistic model of domains should in turn not be restricted to treat domains as independent points in a space. Rather, such a model should be able to walk the domain manifold and adapt to the underlying process that is producing the data.

## 3 Dialogue modeling as a test bed for investigating domains

As a domain presupposes a social component and relies on context, we propose to use dialogue modeling as a test bed to gain a more nuanced understanding of how language varies with domain.

Dialogue modeling can be seen as a prototypical task in natural language processing akin to language modeling and should thus expose variations in the underlying language. It allows one to observe the impact of different strategies to model variation in language across domains on a downstream task, while being inherently unsupervised.

In addition, dialogue has been shown to exhibit characteristics that expose how language changes as conversation partners become more linguistically similar to each other over the course of the conversation (Niederhoffer and Pennebaker, 2002; Levitan et al., 2011). Similarly, it has been shown that the linguistic patterns of individual users in online communities adapt to match those of the community they participate in (Nguyen and Rosé, 2011; Danescu-Niculescu-Mizil et al., 2013).

For this reason, we have selected reddit as a medium and compiled a dataset from large amounts of reddit data. Reddit comments live in a rich environment that is dependent on a large number of contextual factors, such as community, user, conversation, etc. Similar to Chen et al. (2016), we would like to learn representations that allow us to disentangle factors that are normally intertwined, such as style and genre, and that will allow us to gain more insight about the variation in language. To this end, we are currently training models that condition on different communities, users, and threads.

## 4 Representing continuous domains

In line with past research (Daumé III, 2007; Zhou et al., 2016), we assume that every domain has an inherent low-dimensional structure, which allows its

[1] https://en.wikipedia.org/wiki/Yahoo!_Directory

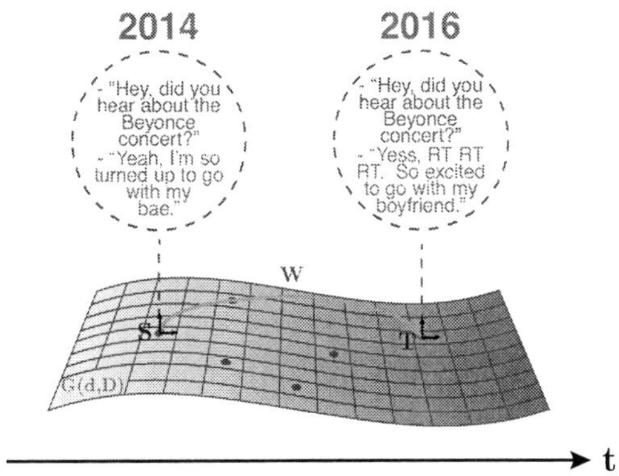


**Figure 1:** Transforming a discrete source domain subspace $S$ into a target domain subspace $T$ with a transformation $W$.

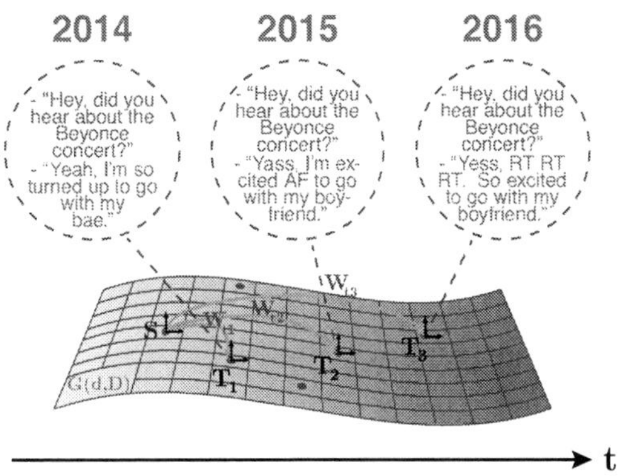


**Figure 2:** Transforming a source domain subspace $S$ into continuous domain subspaces $T_t$ with a temporally varying transformation $W_t$.

projection into a lower dimensional subspace.

In the discrete setting, we are given two domains, a source domain $X_S$ and a target domain $X_T$. We represent examples in the source domain $X_S$ as $x_1^S, \cdots, x_{n_S}^S \in \mathbb{R}^d$ where $x_1^S$ is the $i$-th source example and $n_S$ is number of examples in $X_S$. Similarly, we have $n_T$ target domain examples $x_1^T, \cdots, x_{n_T}^T \in \mathbb{R}^d$.

We now seek to learn a transformation $W$ that allows us to transform the examples in the $X_S$ so that their distribution is more similar to the distribution of $X_T$. Equivalently, we can factorize the transformation $W$ into two transformations $A$ and $B$ with $W = AB^T$ that we can use to project the source and target examples into a joint subspace.

We assume that $X_S$ and $X_T$ lie on lower-dimensional orthonormal subspaces, $S, T \in \mathbb{R}^{D \times d}$, which can be represented as points on the Grassman manifold, $\mathcal{G}(d, D)$ as in Figure 1, where $d \ll D$.

In computer vision, methods such as Subspace Alignment (Fernando et al., 2013) or the Geodesic Flow Kernel (Gong et al., 2012) have been used to find such transformations $A$ and $B$. Similarly, in natural language processing, CCA (Faruqui and Dyer, 2014) and Procrustes analysis (Mogadala and Rettinger, 2016) have been used to align subspaces pertaining to different languages.

Many recent approaches using autoencoders (Bousmalis et al., 2016; Zhou et al., 2016) learn such a transformation between discrete domains. Similarly, in a sequence-to-sequence dialogue model (Vinyals and V. Le, 2015), we can not only train the model to predict the source domain response, but also – via a reconstruction loss – its transformations to the target domain.

For continuous domains, we can assume that source domain $X_S$ and target domain $X_T$ are not independent, but that $X_T$ has evolved from $X_S$ based on a continuous process. This process can be indexed by time, e.g. in order to reflect how a language learner's style changes or how language varies as words rise and drop in popularity. We thus seek to learn a time-varying transformation $W_t$ between $S$ and $T$ that allows us to transform between source and target examples dependent on $t$ as in Figure 2.

Hoffman et al. (2014) assume a stream of observations $z_1, \cdots, z_{n_t} \in \mathcal{R}^d$ drawn from a continuously changing domain and regularize $W_t$ by encouraging the new subspace at $t$ to be close to the previous subspace at $t-1$. Assuming a stream of (chronologically) ordered input data, a straightforward application of this to a representation-learning based dialogue model trains the parts of the model that auto-encode and transform the original message for each new example – possibly regularized with a smoothness constraint – while keeping the rest of the model fixed.

This can be seen as an unsupervised variant of fine-tuning, a common neural network domain adaptation baseline. As our learned transformation continuously evolves, we run the risk associated with fine-tuning of forgetting the knowledge acquired from the source domain. For this reason, neural

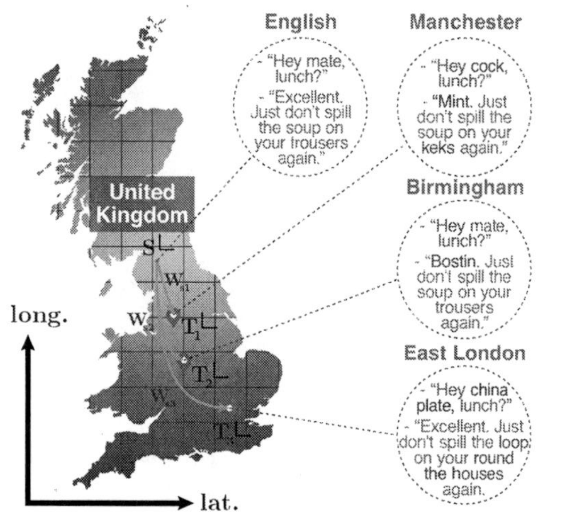


**Figure 3:** Transforming a source domain subspace $S$ into continuous target domain subspaces $T_s$ using a spatially varying transformation $W_s$.

network architectures that are immune to forgetting, such as the recently proposed Progressive Neural Networks (Rusu et al., 2016) are appealing for continuous domain adaptation.

While time is the most obvious dimension along which language evolves, other dimensions are possible: Geographical location influences dialectal variations as in Figure 3; socio-economic status, political affiliation as well as a domain's purpose or complexity all influence language and can thus be conceived as axes that span a manifold for embedding domain subspaces.

## 5 Investigating language change

A continuous notion of domains naturally lends itself to a diachronic study of language. By looking at the representations produced by the model over different time steps, one gains insight into the change of language in a community or another domain. Similarly, observing how a user adapts their style to different users and communities reveals insights about the language of those entities.

Domain mixture models use various domain similarity measures to determine how similar the languages of two domains are, such as Renyi divergence (Van Asch and Daelemans, 2010), Kullback-Leibler (KL) divergence, Jensen-Shannon divergence, and vector similarity metrics (Plank and van Noord, 2011), as well as task-specific measures (Zhou et al., 2016).

While word distributions have been used traditionally to compare domains, embedding domains in a manifold offers the possibility to evaluate the learned subspace representations. For this, cosine similarity as used for comparing word embeddings or KL divergence as used in the Variational Autoencoder (Kingma and Welling, 2013) are a natural fit.

## 6 Evaluation

Our evaluation consists of three parts for evaluating the learned representations, the model, and the variation of language itself.

Firstly, as our models produce new representations for every subspace, we can compare a snapshot of a domain's representation after every $n$ time steps to chart a trajectory of its changes.

Secondly, as we are conducting experiments on dialogue modeling, gold data for evaluation is readily available in the form of the actual response. We can thus train a model on reddit data of a certain period, adapt it to a stream of future conversations and evaluate its performance with BLEU or another metric that might be more suitable to expose variation in language. At the same time, human evaluations will reveal whether the generated responses are faithful to the target domain.

Finally, the learned representations will allow us to investigate the variations in language. Ideally, we would like to walk the manifold and observe how language changes as we move from one domain to the other, similarly to (Radford et al., 2016).

## 7 Conclusion

We have proposed a notion of continuous natural language domains along with dialogue modeling as a test bed. We have presented a representation of continuous domains and detailed how this representation can be incorporated into representation learning-based models. Finally, we have outlined how these models can be used to investigate change and variation in language. While our models allow us to shed light on how language changes, models that can adapt to continuous changes are key for personalization and the reality of grappling with an ever-changing world.

## References


John Blitzer, Ryan McDonald, and Fernando Pereira. 2006. Domain Adaptation with Structural Correspondence Learning. *EMNLP '06 Proceedings of the 2006 Conference on Empirical Methods in Natural Language Processing*, (July):120–128.

Konstantinos Bousmalis, George Trigeorgis, Nathan Silberman, Dilip Krishnan, and Dumitru Erhan. 2016. Domain Separation Networks. *NIPS*.

Xi Chen, Yan Duan, Rein Houthooft, John Schulman, Ilya Sutskever, and Pieter Abbeel. 2016. InfoGAN: Interpretable Representation Learning by Information Maximizing Generative Adversarial Nets. *arXiv preprint arXiv:1606.03657*.

Cristian Danescu-Niculescu-Mizil, Robert West, Dan Jurafsky, and Christopher Potts. 2013. No Country for Old Members : User Lifecycle and Linguistic Change in Online Communities. *Proceedings of the 22nd international conference on World Wide Web*, pages 307–317.

Hal Daumé III and Daniel Marcu. 2006. Domain Adaptation for Statistical Classifiers. *Journal of Artificial Intelligence Research*, 26:101–126.

Hal Daumé III. 2007. Frustratingly Easy Domain Adaptation. *Association for Computational Linguistic (ACL)s*, (June):256–263.

Dan Douglas. 2004. Discourse Domains: The Cognitive Context of Speaking. In Diana Boxer and Andrew D. Cohen, editors, *Studying Speaking to Inform Second Language Learning*. Multilingual Matters.

Manaal Faruqui and Chris Dyer. 2014. Improving Vector Space Word Representations Using Multilingual Correlation. *Proceedings of the 14th Conference of the European Chapter of the Association for Computational Linguistics*, pages 462 - 471.

Basura Fernando, Amaury Habrard, Marc Sebban, Tinne Tuytelaars, K U Leuven, Laboratoire Hubert, Curien Umr, and Benoit Lauras. 2013. Unsupervised Visual Domain Adaptation Using Subspace Alignment. *Proceedings of the IEEE International Conference on Computer Vision*.

Boqing Gong, Yuan Shi, Fei Sha, and Kristen Grauman. 2012. Geodesic Flow Kernel for Unsupervised Domain Adaptation. *2012 IEEE Conference on Computer Vision and Pattern Recognition (CVPR)*.

Judy Hoffman, Trevor Darrell, and Kate Saenko. 2014. Continuous manifold based adaptation for evolving visual domains. *Proceedings of the IEEE Computer Society Conference on Computer Vision and Pattern Recognition*, pages 867–874.

Diederik P Kingma and Max Welling. 2013. Auto-Encoding Variational Bayes. *arXiv preprint arXiv:1312.6114*, (Ml):1–14.

Rivka Levitan, Agustn Gravano, and Julia Hirschberg. 2011. Entrainment in Speech Preceding Backchannels. *Annual Meeting of the Association for Computational Linguistics (ACL/HLT)*, pages 113–117.

Yishay Mansour. 2009. Domain Adaptation with Multiple Sources. *NIPS*, pages 1–8.

David McClosky, Eugene Charniak, and Mark Johnson. 2010. Automatic domain adaptation for parsing. *Human Language Technologies: The 2010 Annual Conference of the North American Chapter of the Association for Computational Linguistics*, pages 28–36.

Aditya Mogadala and Achim Rettinger. 2016. Bilingual Word Embeddings from Parallel and Non-parallel Corpora for Cross-Language Text Classification. *NAACL*, pages 692–702.

Dong Nguyen and Carolyn P. Rosé. 2011. Language use as a reflection of socialization in online communities. *Proceedings of the Workshop on Languages in ...*, (June):76–85.

K. G. Niederhoffer and J. W. Pennebaker. 2002. Linguistic Style Matching in Social Interaction. *Journal of Language and Social Psychology*, 21(4):337–360.

Harriet J. Oppenheimer. 2006. *The Anthropology of Language: An Introduction to Linguistic Anthropology.* Wadsworth, Belmont (Canada).

Sinno Jialin Pan and Qiang Yang. 2010. A survey on transfer learning. *IEEE Transactions on Knowledge and Data Engineering*, 22(10):1345–1359.

Barbara Plank and Gertjan van Noord. 2011. Effective Measures of Domain Similarity for Parsing. *Proceedings of the 49th Annual Meeting of the Association for Computational Linguistics: Human Language Technologies*, 1:1566–1576.

Alec Radford, Luke Metz, and Soumith Chintala. 2016. Unsupervised Representation Learning with Deep Convolutional Generative Adversarial Networks. *ICLR*, pages 1–15.

Andrei A Rusu, Neil C Rabinowitz, Guillaume Desjardins, Hubert Soyer, James Kirkpatrick, Koray Kavukcuoglu, Razvan Pascanu, Raia Hadsell, and Google Deepmind. 2016. Progressive Neural Networks. *arXiv preprint arXiv:1606.04671*.

Vincent Van Asch and Walter Daelemans. 2010. Using Domain Similarity for Performance Estimation. *Computational Linguistics*, (July):31–36.

Oriol Vinyals and Quoc V. Le. 2015. A Neural Conversational Model.

Guangyou Zhou, Zhiwen Xie, Jimmy Xiangji Huang, and Tingting He. 2016. Bi-Transferring Deep Neural Networks for Domain Adaptation. *ACL*, pages 322–332.

# Author Index